James Williamson

The Truth, Inspiration, Authority and Evidence of the Scriptures Considered and Defended

in eight sermons preached before the University of Oxford, in the year MDCCXCIII

James Williamson

The Truth, Inspiration, Authority and Evidence of the Scriptures Considered and Defended
in eight sermons preached before the University of Oxford, in the year MDCCXCIII

ISBN/EAN: 9783337242411

Printed in Europe, USA, Canada, Australia, Japan

Cover: Foto ©Lupo / pixelio.de

More available books at **www.hansebooks.com**

THE TRUTH, INSPIRATION, AUTHORITY, AND END OF THE SCRIPTURES,

CONSIDERED AND DEFENDED,

IN

EIGHT SERMONS,

PREACHED BEFORE THE

UNIVERSITY OF OXFORD,

IN THE YEAR MDCCXCIII.

AT THE

LECTURE

FOUNDED BY THE LATE

REV. JOHN BAMPTON, M.A.

CANON OF SALISBURY.

BY JAMES WILLIAMSON, B.D.
OF QUEEN'S COLLEGE, OXFORD;
PREBENDARY OF LINCOLN, AND RECTOR OF
WINWICK, NORTHAMPTONSHIRE.

OXFORD:

SOLD BY J. COOKE; AND BY G.G. J. AND J. ROBINSON,
AND F. AND C. RIVINGTON, LONDON.
M DCC XCIII.

[Price Four Shillings in Boards.]

IMPRIMATUR,

JOHN WILLS,

Vice-Can. Oxon.

Wadh. Coll. Maii 8, 1793.

TO THE RIGHT REVEREND

AND REVEREND

THE HEADS OF COLLEGES,

THE FOLLOWING SERMONS,

PREACHED

AT THEIR APPOINTMENT,

ARE INSCRIBED,

WITH GREAT RESPECT,

BY THEIR OBEDIENT SERVANT,

THE AUTHOR.

EXTRACT

FROM THE

LAST WILL AND TESTAMENT

OF THE LATE

REV. JOHN BAMPTON,

CANON OF SALISBURY.

―――" I give and bequeath my Lands and
" Eſtates to the Chancellor, Maſters, and
" Scholars of the Univerſity of Oxford for
" ever, to have and to hold all and ſingular
" the ſaid Lands or Eſtates upon truſt, and to
" the intents and purpoſes hereinafter men-
" tioned; that is to ſay, I will and appoint
" that the Vice-Chancellor of the Univerſity
" of Oxford for the time being ſhall take and
" receive

"receive all the rents, issues, and profits
"thereof, and (after all reparations and ne-
"cessary deductions made) that he pay all
"the remainder to the endowment of eight
"Divinity Lecture Sermons, to be establish-
"ed for ever in the said University, and to
"be performed in the manner following:

"I direct and appoint, that, upon the first
"Tuesday in Easter Term, a Lecturer be
"yearly chosen by the Heads of Colleges
"only, and by no others, in the room ad-
"joining to the Printing-House, between
"the hours of ten in the morning and two
"in the afternoon, to preach eight Divinity
"Lecture Sermons, the year following, at St.
"Mary's in Oxford, between the commence-
"ment of the last month in Lent Term, and
"the end of the third week in Act Term.

"Also I direct and appoint, that the eight
"Divinity Lecture Sermons shall be preached
"upon either of the following subjects—to
"confirm and establish the Christian Faith,
"and to confute all heretics and schismatics
 "—upon

"—upon the divine authority of the Holy
"Scriptures — upon the authority of the
"writings of the primitive Fathers, as to
"the faith and practice of the primitive
"Church—upon the Divinity of our Lord
"and Saviour Jesus Christ—upon the Divi-
"nity of the Holy Ghost—upon the Arti-
"cles of the Christian Faith, as compre-
"hended in the Apostles' and Nicene Creeds.

"Also I direct, that thirty copies of the
"eight Divinity Lecture Sermons shall be
"always printed, within two months after
"they are preached, and one copy shall be
"given to the Chancellor of the University,
"and one copy to the Head of every Col-
"lege, and one copy to the Mayor of the
"city of Oxford, and one copy to be put
"into the Bodleian Library; and the ex-
"pence of printing them shall be paid out
"of the revenue of the Land or Estates given
"for establishing the Divinity Lecture Ser-
"mons; and the Preacher shall not be paid,
"nor be entitled to the revenue, before they
"are printed.

"Also

"Also I direct and appoint, that no person shall be qualified to preach the Divinity Lecture Sermons, unless he hath taken the Degree of Master of Arts at least, in one of the two Universities of Oxford or Cambridge; and that the same person shall never preach the Divinity Lecture Sermons twice."

CONTENTS.

SERMON I.

The Importance of Religious Truth.

JOHN xviii. 38.

Pilate saith unto him, What is truth? p. 1

SERMON II.

The Truth of the Scriptures.

JOHN vi. 68.

Then Simon Peter answered him, Lord, to whom shall we go? thou hast the words of eternal life. p. 23

SERMON III.
The Inspiration of the Scriptures.

2 Tim. iii. 16.

All Scripture is given by inspiration of God.

p. 55

SERMON IV.
The Authority of the Scriptures.

John xx. 31.

But these are written, that ye might believe that Jesus is the Christ the Son of God, and that believing ye might have life through his name.

p. 87

SERMON V.
Answer to Objections against Christ's Atonement.

1 John ii. 1, 2.

If any man sin, we have an advocate with the Father, Jesus Christ the righteous: and he is the propitiation for our sins: and not for our sins only, but also for the sins of the whole world.

p. 113

SERMON VI.

The Proofs and Uses of Christ's Atonement.

1 JOHN ii. 1, 2.

If any man sin, we have an advocate with the Father, Jesus Christ the righteous: and he is the propitiation for our sins: and not for our sins only, but also for the sins of the whole world. p. 161

SERMON VII.

The Nature of Faith.

HEBREWS xi. 6.

Without faith it is impossible to please him: for he that cometh to God, must believe that he is, and that he is a rewarder of them that diligently seek him. p. 187

SERMON VIII.

The Necessity of Obedience.

JOHN xiii. 17.

If ye know these things, happy are ye, if ye do them. p. 223

THE IMPORTANCE OF RELIGIOUS TRUTH.

JOHN xviii. 38.

Pilate faith unto him, What is truth?

FROM the behaviour of Pilate, who left the place of judgment immediately after he had afked this queftion, it is very evident, that he neither expected nor defired a fatisfactory anfwer. The variety of opinions, which prevailed in the world, might lead him to conclude, that truth in moft cafes was not eafy to be difcovered. And in the midft of the fchemes of worldly riches and grandeur, he might alfo defpife religious truth, as of little importance. That a Heathen fhould make fuch a falfe and dangerous decifion feems not to be wonderful; but that Chriftians fhould fometimes fhut their eyes againft the cleareft light of reafon and revelation, muft afford matter of serious concern to every sober and considerate mind. All men indeed have not equal abilities or opportunities of cultivating their understanding, and delivering themselves from false principles imbibed in their youth; and all truths are not of the same importance, nor equally easy to be perceived. But though long rooted prejudices have great strength, and it is necessary for the ignorant and unlearned to rely much on the instructions of others; yet if every one would sincerely employ his judgment in searching the grounds of religion without obstinacy or malevolence; though truth might not immediately and universally prevail, we should see men's prejudices vanish by degrees, ancient errors corrected or exploded, and the spirit of Christian unanimity daily increasing.

I shall therefore in my following discourse,

First, shew the importance of religious truth.

Secondly,

Secondly, point out the proper means of discerning, which is true of contradictory assertions. And,

Thirdly, expose the methods, by which artful or bigoted men endeavour to obscure truth, and adorn falshood.

First, I am to shew the importance of religious truth.

Except we are well instructed in religious truth, we shall frequently be ignorant of the nature of God, and our duty towards mankind. The pernicious effects of mistakes in these points upon men's conduct, may be seen in the lives and behaviour of Heathens, Jews, and Christians. By forming wrong notions of the nature of God, the Heathens not only forsook their Creator to worship the host of heaven, and pay divine honours to weak mortals; but, by the attributes and actions, which they ascribed to their false deities, they consecrated the greatest crimes by their example, and supposed them to be pleased and rendered propitious by the most cruel and abominable rites. The Jews in the time of our Saviour had undermined the foundation of filial reverence, and made void by their traditions the most express commands of God. And through excessive zeal, without knowledge, they crucified their long-expected King, and rejected his religion. And even amongst Christians erroneous principles have hardened men's hearts against their brethren, and changed that benevolence, which is declared by our Saviour to be the characteristic mark of his disciples, into bigotry, hatred, envy, and many other bad qualities, which foment divisions. Such being the effect of ignorance and error upon men's religious conduct, we cannot be too careful to furnish our minds by all proper methods with every necessary and important truth.

But if mankind were universally disposed to embrace the truth, and no one had any desire to deceive others, or artfully disguise the falshood of his own opinions, the consequence

sequence would be, that though some might remain ignorant or mistaken in a few points of little importance; yet the light of religious knowledge would rapidly increase, men would speedily apply to the true sources of divine wisdom, and unanimity and benevolence would in course prevail, and pave the way for the entrance of all other virtues. For it is not in this world only that religious truth is useful and necessary; since it has no small influence upon our eternal salvation. Errors in doctrine are seldom harmless: they have a natural tendency to introduce greater, and thus weaken or destroy the chief principles of our faith. Many of them tend likewise to corrupt men's moral conduct. And as far as this is owing to wilfulness or gross negligence, it must hinder in proportion their justification. For though the uncharitable and malicious are apt to think that their zeal will compensate for their mistakes, and that a full persuasion of the rectitude of their opinions, however acquired, will sanctify their most cruel and unjust actions; yet they neither judge thus in the cafe of others, nor will the fupreme Being allow the excufes, by which men palliate or juftify thofe deeds, which they own to be condemned by the general rules of juftice. God has given no one liberty to efpoufe falfhood. And though he will fhew mercy to involuntary ignorance; yet he requires from all that they fhould make ufe of the faculties, which he has beftowed upon them, to difcern the truth, and will feverely punifh fuch as pervert their abilities to deceive others, and impofe upon the fimplicity, credulity, or prejudices of mankind. Thus we may fee that both our prefent and future intereft invite us to cultivate religious truth; fince every error naturally leads to others, and may produce, if not corrected, the moft ferious and fatal confequences to our knowledge, difpofitions, morals, and happinefs. I proceed,

Secondly, to point out the proper means of difcerning, which is true of contradictory affertions.

And

And first, if we are desirous of embracing truth, and rejecting falshood, we should fix in our minds sound principles drawn from proper sources. All real knowledge must proceed from sense, reason, or information. And as religion is much conversant with what is at present invisible, religious wisdom must consist more in giving ear to authentic information, than in our own experience or uncertain conjectures. We must therefore, in order to be wise unto salvation, employ our reason, with modesty and humility, to discern the authenticity and discover the sense of divine revelation; and give up ourselves to be guided by the will of God, notwithstanding the opposition of our depraved nature.

And if we desire to find out the truth, we should cultivate our reason by all the means in our power. We should endeavour to acquire an habitual readiness in classing every subject in its proper place, in discovering all its qualities, and discerning which are to be esteemed properties, and which acci-

accidental; in diftinguifhing between realities and appearances; and giving its due weight to every argument on either fide of a queftion. Though this might be performed to a great degree by a frequent exertion of our own natural powers; yet it may tend to accelerate this ufeful work, to fupply deficiencies, and to prevent miftakes, if we add the help of fome artificial fyftem, and unite the wifdom of our anceftors with our own abilities. It is true that this art has formerly been difgraced by being employed upon ufelefs fubjects, and often made the inftrument of defending falfhood, rather than difcovering the truth. But this affords no juft argument againft the improvement of our reafon; fince there is nothing in this world, however excellent, which cannot be abufed to the purpofes of folly and vice. He is moft likely to form a juft conclufion, who habitually views objects in a true light, and depends more or lefs upon his own underftanding, according to the opportunities he has had to be well informed. But though the ufe of fome fyftem may prevent the
wan-

wanderings of our imagination; yet we should not be so bigoted to any particular method, as to think it a key to the reasoning of all ages and nations. There may be some difficulty to understand the meaning and full force of ancient arguments, if we do not rightly observe what propositions were omitted, as so evidently true in the opinion of both parties, as not to require to be proved, or even mentioned.

Lastly, if we desire to embrace the truth, let us clear our minds of all prejudices, that have any tendency to lead us astray. When by education we have contracted a love for any society or persons, we are inclined to palliate their faults, and to entertain a favourable opinion of all their doctrines. And if we are bred up to hate or despise our adversaries, we shall in like manner be induced to detract from their virtues, and disallow their judgment. Hence arise sects and parties, who are ready to be convinced in some cases by the weakest arguments, and in others to withstand the strongest proofs.

proofs. But though we should examine every doctrine according to our abilities, and not believe any thing merely because we were taught it before we arrived at the full use of our understanding; yet we are not to be lukewarm in religion, or reject without distinction the opinions of our former years. For when we are commanded to *prove all things,* we are ordered likewise to *hold fast that which is good.* A candid examination may often convince us, that we have been well instructed from our youth. A habit of doubting therefore, carried too far, is equally dangerous with implicit confidence. Truth, then, should always excite our zeal according to its importance, whether it agrees or disagrees with our present tenets, and whether we are indebted for it to the information of others, or our own discovery. I proceed,

Thirdly, to expose the methods, by which artful or bigoted men endeavour to obscure truth, and adorn falshood.

One method, by which men recommend falshood

falshood in preference to truth, is by positive assertions of false principles or pretended facts, and contempt or ridicule of what are true. Weak and ignorant persons are ready to believe, without proof, what they hear asserted by those of superior knowledge and understanding, provided it neither injures their temporal interest, nor contradicts their desires. Hence we often see in controversy very doubtful propositions taken for granted, unsupported facts boldly asserted, credible testimony slighted or denied, and important truths treated with contempt. The mischief arising from this practice is very extensive; as innumerable false conclusions may be drawn from erroneous principles and mistaken facts, and men are with difficulty convinced, that they have hitherto been deceived in what they looked upon as axioms and uncontroverted truths.

But though men will, in support of their opinions, however false and prejudicial, proceed sometimes to inconceivable lengths; yet in general they are more artful, and leave
their

their readers to draw false conclusions from insinuations founded upon premises partly true, or facts that are misrepresented and distorted in their circumstances. The connection between two propositions is not always perceived. Hence men may impose upon the simple by shewing what conclusion they would wish to form, and producing as an argument, what is in some sense true, or not easy to be confuted; though in the sense required by just reasoning it is entirely false, or has little or no reference to the subject in debate.

And as many propositions are neither universally true, nor universally false; deceivers often impose upon the weak by making them believe that to be universally true, which is so only in some particular circumstances. In morality, the relation, situation, and other circumstances of an agent create a considerable difference in the nature of some actions, which appear similar to an inattentive observer. In societies likewise free will and the various dispositions of

mankind

mankind cause them, when influenced by the strictest connections, to act in a different manner, though impelled by the same outward motives. We shall therefore be liable to error and delusion, if we neglect to mark every circumstance, upon which depends the truth or falshood of any proposition; or if we praise, blame, or excuse the conduct of a society in general for the good or bad behaviour of a few individuals.

And even when men ascribe particular qualities to their proper subjects, they may deceive the unwary by representing them better or worse than they really are. When we praise the goodness of an action, or the justness of an opinion, the good may be exaggerated, or the necessary limitations overlooked. And in like manner, where there is some ground for blame, the censure may be too severe on the one hand, or the fault too much palliated on the other. Thus, when we hear the same action related by a friend and an enemy, the degree of good or evil is often so increased or diminished by favour or hatred, that every impartial perfon may eafily perceive, that one or both opinions muſt be very far diſtant from the real truth.

Another method of deceiving is, by a change of the fubject, to put the refemblance for the reality, and thus obtain praife or procure blame for what deferves the reverfe. The motive, means, or manner of an action often contribute much to its goodnefs, or enhance its guilt. The fame action may be virtuous or vicious, as it agrees with the will of God and the happinefs of our neighbour, or is attended with fuch circumſtances, as contradict his laws, and violate the duties of civil fociety. By difregarding thefe diſtinctions, the name of liberty has frequently been ufed for a cloak of malicioufnefs, a juſt feparation from the corruptions of a tyrannical church is branded with the crime of herefy and fchifm, and hypocrify of various kinds has been recommended and dignified with the name of religion.

But

But a still more fruitful source of error consists in an application to the passions to determine difficulties, instead of submitting them to the decision of reason. A man under the influence of interest or inclination, often shuts his eyes against the light, and rejects every evidence below the testimony of his senses, which tends to refute his favourite mistake. It is almost incredible, if it were not proved both by history and experience, to what absurdities men's passions will excite them; and how often by the force of prejudice they believe the most unlikely facts upon weak evidence, and reject what is not only probable in itself, but confirmed by the testimony of impartial witnesses.

When these methods of deceit have been successful any time, they prepare the way to an implicit faith in men's persons, which affords the most dangerous and extensive means of spreading erroneous notions. It is true, that a wise and good teacher would, if implicitly followed, lead his disciples into the

the way of holiness. But still implicit faith in men's religious opinions, without respect to their conformity with some superior rule, is neither useful nor safe; as it exposes us to be led astray by the folly and wickedness of the presumptuous or artful. A good man would desire, that his followers should know, as far as they are capable, the grounds of their faith. And it is more his wish and endeavour, that they should profit in religion, than be attached to his person. The lower and more ignorant part of mankind must to a certain degree be guided by their superiors in knowledge, to prevent the ill effects of their own mistakes. But this confidence should be founded upon their integrity, and not extended to those instances, where all are plainly capable of judging for themselves, and can see the doctrines of their teachers contradicted by superior authority.

As therefore it is sometimes prudent to follow, and sometimes to reject, the opinions of others; deceivers endeavour to gain the admiration of their followers by the appearance

ance of wisdom and holiness, or condescend to the mean art of flattering their passions, and exciting their pride. At the same time they frequently prejudice their minds against the true doctrines of religion, by a malicious aggravation of the faults of their opponents, by ridicule and contempt of their persons, or illiberal abuse of their practices and opinions. And we need not wonder, that such arts are used, in these days, to render contemptible the regular and orthodox ministers of God, and that they sometimes meet with success, when we are told in Scripture, that the authority of St. Paul, who was endowed with a variety of supernatural gifts, was despised by some of the Corinthians, because his bodily presence seemed mean, and his speech contemptible.

And as we must rely upon testimony for the knowledge of facts, which we have not seen, and doctrines, which reason alone cannot fully discover; another door is opened for deceit, if the nature and extent of this testimony is misrepresented or mistaken.

The proof of such facts and doctrines depends upon their delivery, by credible authors, in terms sufficiently plain; and if they are not thus supported, they may be safely disbelieved.

A negative argument then, to have due force, requires a total silence of all credible authors upon the subject in dispute. And it is evidently a weak or false conclusion, though it may impose upon the prejudiced and ignorant, to doubt or deny a doctrine supported by clear testimony, because it is not mentioned in some particular places, is not repeated more than once or twice, and is not delivered in a certain mode of expression. This method of reasoning in religious affairs would subject revelation to the caprice, obstinacy, and perverseness of man, and make our weak reason a competent judge of the wisdom and rectitude of the divine proceedings. To conceal therefore wilfully any material passages, to weaken the force of others by trifling objections, or to reverse the meaning of any sentence by an imperfect

imperfect quotation, are arts, which betray a consciousness of an unsound cause, and give reason to suspect, that the person who employs them is more eager to pursue victory than truth.

But whatever arts men use to pervert the truth and recommend falshood, the former is so simple, amiable, useful, and consistent, and the latter so pernicious and full of contradictions, that the most bigoted minds would be frequently undeceived, if they were permitted to judge fairly of the different pretensions of such as desire to instruct them in religion. Hence impostors and deceivers, and even persons who are themselves mistaken, commonly deliver their falsest assertions in such general or equivocal terms, use such a vague latitude in their concessions and limitations, and leave their meaning, where it ought most to be explained, in such uncertainty, that they can elude the force of a direct charge, and represent their antagonist as guilty of a malicious accusation. The supporters of truth are thus looked upon as deceivers, and expoſed to the diſgrace that belongs to falſhood.

Obſcurity is indeed ſo favourable to falſhood, that we often find the firſt attempt to propagate falſe doctrines undertaken with caution. They are for a time rather dropt in hints, than aſſerted in form; and repreſented as harmleſs opinions, than inſiſted on as neceſſary truths. But when they have eſcaped contradiction by being thus diſguiſed; the maſk is thrown off by degrees, and at laſt they are aſſumed as maxims too evident to need any poſitive proof, and which cannot be denied without the loſs of our claim to judgment, candour, learning, and common ſenſe. The proper teſts of truth are thus overlooked and deſpiſed, and the deciſion of the moſt important queſtions made to depend upon the arts of ſophiſtry, the pretenſions of confidence, and the prevalence of the paſſions of the weak and ignorant.

Since then truth is the guide to happineſs, both here and hereafter, and all falſhood

hood is inconsistent with the purity of God, let us withdraw our confidence from every teacher, and guard against his arts, who wilfully endeavours to misrepresent or conceal the truth; and let us not only resolve to avoid the use of all fraud and deceit, but so cultivate our reason, and improve our judgment, that we may likewise escape all mistakes and delusions.

THE TRUTH OF THE SCRIPTURES.

John vi. 68.

Then Simon Peter answered him, Lord, to whom shall we go? thou hast the words of eternal life.

WHEN we consider the shortness of human life, we must naturally be anxious to know what state will succeed, and by what means we may secure eternal happiness. Philosophy could discover the probability, that death would not terminate man's existence; it could shew the excellence of virtue, and likewise the propriety of a future distinction between the righteous and the wicked. But unassisted reason must have many doubts and difficulties concerning heavenly doctrines. Revelation alone could declare with certainty the true nature of God, the extent of our duty, and the means of being justified and admitted to a state of purity and bliss. The Holy Scriptures, which were finished by the doctrines of our Lord and his Apostles, profess to contain this revelation. And when we consider their superiority over the claims of pretenders to inspiration, the ancient systems of human wisdom, or the boasted light of modern philosophy, we may well say in the words of my text, *Lord, to whom shall we go? thou hast the words of eternal life.* I shall therefore in my following discourse endeavour to establish the truth of the Holy Scriptures,

First, by shewing the external evidence, that they contain the revealed will of God. And,

Secondly, by considering the internal marks of their truth and authenticity, which may be discovered in their composition. And

First, I am to shew the external evidence, that the Scriptures contain the revealed will of God.

As

As the Holy Scriptures were conveyed to the world by the hands of men, and not visibly sent down by an angel from heaven, it was proper, and almost necessary, that they should be proved to contain the word of God by some external evidence, and not rely entirely upon the credibility of their writers, or their own intrinsic excellence. Accordingly the publication both of the Old and New Testament was attended by numerous and stupendous miracles, by which God manifestly declared his concurrence, and added his sanction. And during the Mosaic dispensation, he occasionally shewed his power in the same manner for the protection of innocence, the defence of his people, or the vindication of his honour. The Scripture miracles are a convincing proof of a divine commission. Every effect must be produced by a proportionable cause. When, therefore, we see a work that exceeds the ordinary powers of nature, its author must be some intelligent being; and if it be impossible to be wrought by any creature, without supernatural assistance, it must necessarily

cessarily be ascribed to the operation of the Almighty, or his commissioned agents. This reasoning seems both plain and forcible; adapted to the level of the weakest and most uncultivated understanding, and not to be denied by the most learned, if free from prejudice, or evaded by the most acute. A late infidel writer * has indeed endeavoured to represent all miracles as incredible, under the notion that every fact, which contradicts experience, is opposed by as strong testimony, as is brought in it's support.

But here it should be observed, that a miracle does not contradict experience in such a manner, as to demonstrate that either of them is false. Reason teaches, that a natural cause acting in the same circumstances will always be followed by the same effect. But the longest and most uniform experience will by no means prove, that a different or even a contrary effect may not be produced by a different cause. A miracle is not pretended to be wrought by natural causes. The proof therefore of its reality

* Hume.

arises

arises partly from the evidence of men's senses, that such an effect is produced, and partly from experimental knowledge, that the powers of nature are not able to perform such a work alone. Unless, therefore, we deny the power of God to direct and controul the laws of nature, or suppose, without proof, that he has bound himself never (for any reason) to make the least alteration, we must grant miracles to be possible in themselves; and need only examine, whether those recorded in Scripture be worthy of God, and consequently credible, as requiring his hand, being wrought for an end agreeable to his will, upon occasions sufficiently important, submitted to the plain sense and reason of the beholders, and delivered to posterity upon strong and impartial testimony. The miracles recorded in Scripture were great, and required the concurrence of the God of Nature. Moses shewed that he could direct and controul the elements, and our Saviour not only cured the most obstinate diseases, but displayed an absolute authority over the grave and the powers of darkness.

darkness. They were likewise, in general, publicly wrought before friends and enemies, attended with some declaration or sign, that such an effect would be produced, and performed in so short a time, as precluded all possibility of contrivance or deceit. Their end also was worthy of a just, merciful, and beneficent God. They were designed to punish atrocious offenders, to protect the innocent, to give credit to the prophets, or to introduce a religious dispensation. If the instruction of mankind in religious knowledge be a sufficient reason for God to bestow and confirm a revelation of his will, and the dignity of Christ with the end of his coming be of such importance, that they deserve to be proved by all kinds of evidence, the miracles of the Old and New Testament were not wrought in vain, or for a cause unworthy of divine interference.

But it may be objected, that of whatever force the testimony of miracles might be to those, by whom they were seen, they come to us with diminished authority. To this it may

may be answered, that if we have credible evidence of their being really wrought, they are a sufficient foundation for our belief, though in this case we walk by faith, and not by sight. The age of our Saviour and his Apostles was famous for learning; yet their miracles were not only acknowledged by the converts to christianity, from Jewish prejudices and Heathen superstitions; but the reality of the facts was allowed even by their adversaries, who, after full opportunities of discerning the truth, and sufficient motives to make them eager to detect the least deceit, ascribed them to magic, or some other inadequate or improbable cause. And if we grant the existence of our Saviour's miracles, the rest, mentioned in the Old Testament, are not only supported by the uniform tradition of the Jewish nation, but confirmed by the testimony of him and his disciples.

Another external proof of the truth of the Scriptures is prophecy. As miracles are chiefly adapted to the age, in which they are

are wrought, and can have no farther weight with succeeding generations, than as they are authenticated by sensible, honest, and unprejudiced witnesses: so prophecy is suited to convince those, who see its predictions fulfilled; and, when first delivered, can only have the effect of a solemn appeal to God, which will be of greater or less weight according to the prudence and moral character of the prophet. Indeed, as prophecies may be fulfilled at different periods, a prophet may obtain honour, even in his life, if he foretells what is accomplished at a short distance; provided the event is too obscure to be discovered by human wisdom, or too difficult to be compassed by human contrivance. In this case the evidence of divine assistance, in one instance, forms a sufficient assurance, that it will not fail in another. And such an argument cannot be overthrown or rejected by a sound reasoner, unless a prophecy, which relies upon equal or similar authority, should be proved to have evidently failed. In like manner, when we see with our own eyes some remarkable and important

portant predictions, confessedly delivered many centuries past, at this time fulfilling without the concurrence of men's secular interest, we have not only a proof from thence of the truth of Christianity and the Holy Scriptures, but may firmly believe, that all those, which are recorded in the same books, really came to pass in their respective seasons; as none of them are disproved by contemporary writers. The prophecies of Scripture frequently contained circumstances very unlikely to happen at the time of their delivery; and were either beyond the power of the prophet to effect by natural means, if they were to be fulfilled soon, or their accomplishment was deferred so long, that his authority, influence, and connections must have been entirely dissolved. They were often, likewise, attended with circumstances seemingly contradictory till explained by the event, and some of them so casual, that they could only be noticed in due season by that Providence, which sees at one view all that will come to pass from the beginning to the end of the world.

The

The prophecy of Elisha, that the city would be rescued from a most grievous famine in the space of one day, must have overwhelmed him with shame, if he had not been divinely inspired. And an impostor, who had trusted to chance alone, would never have added, that the unbelieving lord, who was thus forewarned, should live to see the truth of the prediction, and yet not enjoy the common deliverance. The prophecy to Jeroboam, the first king of Israel, that his altar should be destroyed by some future king of Judah, considering the civil and religious enmity between the two kingdoms, might have been hazarded without any claim to superior wisdom, if it had been generally delivered without any limitation. But when we read, that it was to be fulfilled by a child born to the house of Judah, named Josiah, and find it accomplished at the distance of three hundred years, we see the hand of God evidently displayed. Josiah was named, when his disposition was not known. He reigned eighteen years before he attempted to destroy idolatry. His life was short. And except he had been divinely conducted in his undertakings, he might easily have omitted the destruction of this altar. The former kings of Judah had no authority in the land of Israel. And the power of his successors was soon diminished, till the whole nation was led into captivity. When therefore we see only one Josiah amongst all the kings of Judah, who fulfilled this prophecy without any particular knowledge or intention, the hand of God is remarkably evident in disposing the events of this world in such a manner, as may display at once both his power and his providence.

The prophecies concerning the fate of Babylon, Tyre, Jerusalem, and Egypt, are of such a nature, as could not have been hazarded upon mere conjecture without a manifest probability of failure and detection. That they are as ancient as they pretend, we have neither reason nor authority to entertain a doubt. And though cities and kingdoms are liable to decay; yet that proud Babylon

Babylon should fall from its highest grandeur within seventy years, was a fact, that could only be foreknown by the divine wisdom. The agreement of these prophecies with the present state of the world is equally clear. Babylon is so completely a pool of water, according to the words of Isaiah and Jeremiah, that its very ruins cannot be discovered. Tyre, whose merchants were princes, is now a miserable habitation for fishermen. Jerusalem is still trodden down of the Gentiles. And Egypt, which was famous for wisdom, riches, and power, continues a base kingdom, and has been in abject slavery many hundred years.

The Arabians afford likewise a strong instance of the truth of the Scripture prophecies. That Ishmael should be a wild man, his hand against every man, and every man's hand against him, and yet dwell in the presence of all his brethren, are circumstances, which were never found consistent for any length of time, except in the case of the Arabians and the Romans. It is the most
unlikely

unlikely of a people, situated in the centre of the world, and near to powerful and civilized nations. Yet we neither find by history, that they were ever completely conquered by the Persians or Romans, nor do we see their independence lessened to this very day.

But the dispersion of the Jews is a prophecy most convincing to our senses; because it was the latest delivered, is visible in all nations, and has been continued without intermission from the age of the Apostles to the present time. This is likewise the strongest proof of the truth of our Saviour's pretensions, when we see that God for his death and rejection has so severely punished his chosen people; whom he yet preserves, and promises to restore, in remembrance of his covenant with Abraham, Isaac, and Jacob. This judgment should make us careful not to imitate their infidelity. And their relation to God by adoption should make us pity, rather than despise, their hardness of heart.

It may be observed concerning prophecies, especially of great importance, that they are mostly obscure before the event. If they had been otherwise, their enemies must often have been restrained by a miracle from attempting to hinder their accomplishment; and their friends would sometimes have disgraced their Divine original by striving to fulfil them by human contrivance. And even after the event we may in some find small circumstances, which cannot be proved entirely to correspond. If the fact be conveyed to us by history, every minute particular may not be recorded. And if we see it with our own eyes, we may not accurately observe things, which are of less moment; or we may possibly be mistaken in our interpretation. It should therefore be esteemed sufficient, that the great outlines of every prophecy be clear to all capacities, that we see no part evidently contradicted, and that there be such a correspondence between the prediction and the event, as could not be discovered by human wisdom, or brought about by human power.

And

And here it seems proper to take notice of an objection * lately urged to the prophecy concerning the Jews, that our Saviour " decisively foretold, that the genera-
" tion then existing should not be totally
" extinguished, till it had witnessed his se-
" cond and glorious appearance in the clouds
" of heaven." Our Saviour's prophecy concerning the punishment of the Jews, and his second coming to judge the world, is partly accomplished in the destruction of Jerusalem and the dispersion of the nation, partly we see it fulfilling before our eyes in the present state of the Israelites, and partly we perceive it not yet fulfilled, as the world still continues, though we firmly expect Christ to be our judge. When we see so much of this prophecy distinctly and wonderfully fulfilled, and have such abundant testimony that Christ will hereafter come in the glory of his Father with his holy angels, we should rather think that the words, which respect the time of this event, ought to be understood in

* Dr. Edwards, in a Sermon preached before the University of Cambridge, May 23, 1790. p. 19, l. 17.

some other sense, which at the last day will be proved consistent with the rest, than that our Saviour and his Apostles were either mistaken themselves, or taught their followers what they did not know to be true. When it is said in St. Matthew, (xvi. 28.) *Verily I say unto you, there be some standing here, which shall not taste of death, till they see the Son of Man coming in his kingdom,* it does not follow, though this sentence be closely connected with the mention of the day of judgment, that by coming in his kingdom our Saviour meant to describe his most solemn and glorious act of royalty. His kingdom commenced at his resurrection; and he may in a very fit sense be said to be seen coming in his kingdom, whenever we see his power displayed in any signal act of vengeance upon his enemies, though he is not at that time personally visible. The rule here laid down by the author of this objection for the interpretation of words is not universally and strictly true. "Whenever," says he, * "the same word is used in the same

* P. 14, l. 3.

" sentence,

" sentence, or in different sentences not dis-
" tant from each other, we ought to inter-
" pret it precisely in the same sense; unless
" either that sense should involve a palpable
" contradiction of ideas, or the writer ex-
" pressly informs us that he repeats the word
" in a fresh acceptation." Almost every word has many different meanings, and is used in each meaning with more or less latitude in different passages. Without, therefore, any contradiction of ideas or express declaration of the writer, we may judge that he uses the same word not *precisely* in the same sense, if the subject or the context warrant such an interpretation. And as the word *see* is frequently used for perceive, when no bodily appearance is mentioned, we may grant that Christ did not visibly appear at the destruction of Jerusalem, without giving up our belief in him as a true prophet, or our hopes that he will at the last day be the judge and rewarder of his faithful followers. The signal overthrow of the Jewish kingdom, and the vengeance executed on God's chosen people, are events of such import-

importance, as may well be defcribed in the boldeft language of prophecy. The ufe, therefore, of fuch fublime images, as in their literal fenfe would figure the deftruction of the world, is not (as this author afferts) " to embarrafs revelation with perplexities " or contradictions, or to involve it in Cim- " merian darknefs." We have feen the punifhment of the Jews for their rejection of Chrift, and we are thence cautioned to beware, that there be not found in any of us an evil heart of unbelief. As long then as the gates of hell cannot prevail for the extinction of chriftianity; fo long we fhall expect, that he will in due feafon fulfil his words, and finally triumph over all his enemies. For though we now only know in part; yet at the laft day we fhall know even as we are known, and fee the truth and confiftency of all God's difpenfations.

" The predictions of the Apoftles con-
" cerning the end of the world," are alfo faid*
" to furnifh examples of confiderable error."

* P. 11, l. 5.

But

But it does not appear, that they *knew the times and the seasons, which the Father hath put in his own power*; (Acts i. 7.) or that they had any authority, when they preached the gospel, to define the time of the general judgment. An exhortation, therefore, not to be overtaken by the suddenness of Christ's coming ought not to be converted into a decisive prediction, that this event would happen in that very generation. The epistles, though directed to the Christians then alive, were intended for the edification of the church to the end of the world. Whatever therefore is said to them, may be understood to be said to all; and St. Paul's description of the manner of our change at the day of judgment may be applied to the Christians, who shall be then alive. The same may be observed concerning St. Peter's caution (1 Pet. iv. 7.) *to be sober*, because *the end of all things is at hand*; and St. Paul's remark to the Hebrews, that they could *see the day approaching*. (Heb. x. 25.) St. Paul in his second Epistle warns the Thessalonians *not to be troubled, as if the day of Christ was very near*;

(2 Thess.

(2 Theff. ii. 2.) fince that day fhould not come, *till the man of fin was revealed.* (ii. 3.) And though this expreffion does not pofitively affirm, that it was at any confiderable diftance; yet the defcription of the man of fin agrees very well with a fyftem of fpiritual corruption, how long foever it may continue. St. Peter alfo informs us, that *there shall come in the laſt days, ſcoffers, ſaying, Where is the promiſe of his coming?* (2 Pet. iii. 3, 4.) To this he anſwers, *Beloved, be not ignorant of this one thing, that one day is with the Lord as a thouſand years, and a thouſand years as one day. The Lord is not ſlack concerning his promiſe, as ſome men count ſlackneſs.* (iii. 8, 9.) We may therefore conclude, that the coming of our Lord is certain, though it may feem to be delayed; and though fome parts of his prediction may be difficult to be explained at prefent, yet we may reft aſſured that *heaven and earth ſhall paſs away, but his words ſhall not paſs away.* (Matt. xxiv. 25.)

Another proof of the truth of the Scriptures

tures may be taken from the character of the writers. Moses was learned in all the wisdom of the Egyptians, and therefore not to be imposed upon by rumours and false opinions. He has the testimony of the author of the Epistle to the Hebrews, that he was *faithful to God* (iii. 2.) in the discharge of his office. From which we may conclude, that the law, which he imposed upon his people, was of divine original, and that he could not be guilty of mixing falshoods with important truths, or giving rash conjectures for authentic history. His character has not been aspersed by any ancient author of credit; and even the impostor Mahomet found his memory so much revered by the Jews, that he acknowledged his claim as a prophet, though he asserted without proof, that his writings had been corrupted. The prophets likewise, who, besides the books which bear their names, are supposed to have written the historical part of the Old Testament, were men in general of religion and morality, sent to recall the people from sin and idolatry, and what

puts

puts the matter out of all difpute, quoted by our Saviour and his Apoftles as teachers of the way of God, and many of them fufferers in the caufe of truth. The actions indeed of Solomon were not always conformable to his knowledge. But his wifdom is undifputed. And therefore his authority, except in the cafe of idolatry, muft be ftrong in favour of religion, which he has proved in general to be the road to happinefs, even in the prefent world. *Her ways are ways of pleafantnefs, and all her paths are peace. She is a tree of life to them that lay hold upon her; and happy is every one that retaineth her.* (Prov. iii. 17, 18.) Our Saviour indeed was the only perfon that could fay without the leaft exception, *Which of you convinceth me of fin?* (John viii. 46.) But the Apoftles and Evangelifts were holy and wife, and could therefore ftamp an authority upon their writings, even if they had not moft of them fealed their fincerity with their blood, and if their hiftorical accounts had not been confirmed, as far as can be expected, by profane hiftory. I proceed,

Secondly,

Secondly, to confider the internal marks of truth and authenticity, which may be difcovered in the compofition of the Scriptures.

When we compare the natural abilities and fituation of the Apoftles with the doctrines and precepts of the gofpel, it is certain that in their excellence we may perceive evident marks of divine affiftance. The morality is pure and complete, and fuperior to the efforts of human wifdom aided by ftudy and inftruction. For though the principal duties of morality are implanted in every man's breaft, and may be all found difperfed amongft the writings of the philofophers; yet they were delivered by the Apoftles, who were moftly illiterate, in a more excellent and ufeful manner. The precepts of the Gofpel point out the feveral duties of life in their full extent, without any encouragement of vice, or mixture of falfhood. They are founded upon the plaineft and moft engaging principles, and guarded with the fevereft fanctions againft wilful offenders,

offenders, and the moft gracious promifes to the penitent and obedient. We are commanded to make our own reafonable defires the rule of our conduct towards others; to fhew that kindnefs, mercy, and compaffion to our fellow creatures, to which we are indebted for our prefent life and future profpects; and to confider all men as of the fame family, and therefore naturally united in the bands of friendfhip. All thefe precepts are fo confiftent with each other, and the practice of every virtue fo neceffary to a holy life, that the Chriftian fyftem is proved worthy of God; though it would never have been collected by human wifdom alone, or obeyed by our prefent depraved paffions without the divine influence of inward grace.

But the conduct of our Saviour is urged by a modern author againft all attempts of giving a clear and comprehenfive view of the principal doctrines and duties of chriftianity. " Another remarkable characteriftic of chrif- " tianity," fays he*, "is its fimplicity." This

* Effays Phil. Hift. and Lit. vol. i. p. 420.

we

we both grant and boast of, as it proves the wisdom of its author, who could form a religion containing so many duties in such a manner, that they should all spring from the same root, that it should be so well connected in all its parts, and that so many persons, in distant ages, should describe various and yet consistent characters of the same Messiah. A system may be simple, as well as complex. And therefore neither this circumstance, nor the other, " that our Saviour left no records, " or written memorials, respecting the end " and object of his mission," tends any thing " to the utter confusion of systems " or system-makers." Our Saviour certainly came into the world for some important end. He never meant, that the knowledge of the Gospel should be confined to a single age, and posterity remain without information. He left, it is true, no writings of his own. But this is neither an *astonishing fact*, nor any condemnation of well grounded systems; since he sent his Apostles into all the world to be his witnesses, and to preach the Gospel, from whose accounts of his life and

and doctrine we have sufficient materials to learn the nature of our duty, which we are no where forbidden to commit to memory in any manner consistent with the truth. St. Paul informs us what is the true foundation of all systems of religion: *Other foundation can no man lay, than that is laid, which is Jesus Christ.* (1 Cor. iii. 11.) And in the following verses he mentions the different event of building properly or improperly upon this foundation. *If any man's work abide, which he hath built thereupon, he shall receive a reward. If any man's work shall be burnt, he shall suffer loss.* (14, 15.) To preach the true doctrines of religion, and to turn many to righteousness, is undoubtedly acceptable in the sight of God. And we need not be afraid of drawing true conclusions from the Scriptures; but of obscuring the truth, or promoting falsehoods. The sum and substance of the Christian religion does not consist in the facts of our Saviour's life, death, resurrection, and second coming to judge the world, though we believe the truth and importance of all these articles;

unless

unless we join with them the design of his sufferings, the obligation we are under to follow his bright example, and the virtues, which we are called upon to exercise, and to the performance of which is annexed the promise of our future reward.

But it is farther objected, that " no au-
" thentic account of our Saviour's life was
" published till a considerable time after his
" resurrection; and even then, not by any
" previous or express commission from him,
" but to gratify the laudable desire of the
" numerous proselytes to this new religion;"
and that " the Christian religion subsisted
" long before St. Paul wrote his celebrated
" Epistles." This has the appearance of a wish to lessen the authority of both the Epistles and the Gospels; though it calls the former celebrated, and the desire laudable of perusing the latter. And surely it is equally laudable in us to be eager to know the particulars of our Lord's life and conversation, as it was in the first christians. But though we have no express order of our
Saviour

Saviour for committing his life and doctrines to writing; yet when he gave his disciples a command to preach the gospel to the whole world, they were fully justified in taking the most effectual way for the information of posterity. And though they might be desired to write the Gospels, it by no means follows, that they intended to teach and gratify no others, than those, who lived in the same age, and had the benefit of their discourses. The words and acts of our Saviour were published from the beginning. And if St. Paul wrote the same doctrines, they are not to be neglected, because they had before been spoken by our Lord and his Apostles. Preaching is intended not only to instruct mankind in what they do not know; but to prevent them from forgetting useful truths. And it is not only evident, that writing is a more probable method of conveying doctrines pure to distant generations, than tradition; but we have good reason to think, that the latter alone would before this time have lost most of the facts of our Saviour's life, and some of the peculiar doctrines

trines of the Christian religion. We should therefore equally esteem the necessary and useful writings of the Apostles and Evangelists, when composed at the latter end of their ministry, as if they had been published at the beginning, whilst they contain the same truths. For if we are inclined to reject the doctrines of the inspired writers for such slight causes, we may never want a pretence for disavowing their authority.

The truth of the Scripture is also proved internally by the agreement of all its parts with right reason, as far as they can be at present comprehended, and their consistency with each other. Fable and imposture commonly betray themselves by some detected falshood, or manifest contradiction. Whereas the adversaries of christianity are obliged to distort the doctrines, and misrepresent the facts, of the Old and New Testament, before they can persuade even themselves, that they are false or absurd. The length of time, which the scheme of christianity required, the variety of its parts, and the number

number of prophets and other perfons, who contributed their affiftance independent of each other, all confpired to make deception difficult. And the final accomplifhment by means naturally fo inadequate amounts to a demonftration that it proceeded from above. The Scriptures contain the only articles, which concern the whole world; man's creation, fall, and redemption. Their account of the power, knowledge, purity, juftice, and mercy of God is far beyond the inventions of poets, or the difcoveries of philofophers amongft the Heathen, where they were not affifted by accidental hints from divine revelation. And if we defcend to the hiftory of mankind, it is much more reafonable to fuppofe, that man was created innocent, perfect, and happy, than to imagine with fome of the Heathen poets and orators, that he was deftitute of all conveniencies, deprived of fpeech, and refcued from thofe evils by the ufe of that reafon and eloquence, which can fcarcely be cultivated, except in fociety. Such a ftate is unfit for the firft fituation of the only reafonable sonable animal; and if it had ever been universal, must naturally have been attended with the destruction of a species, the individuals of which are so weak, and subject to such a long and helpless infancy. The general promise also of our redemption was given at the fall, opened by degrees with various circumstances, and fulfilled at last by a single person. The several distances between Abraham, Moses, the Prophets, and Christ destroy all suspicion of any collusion. And the concurrence of all the prophecies in the person of our Saviour prove that he came from God to fulfil his will.

Since then the Holy Scriptures are proved to be the word of God by a variety of the strongest evidence; since both the law and the gospel were ushered in by a number of well authenticated miracles; since the doctrines they teach are sublime, pure, and beneficial; since the characters of their authors are able to stamp a credit upon any writings; since they are so closely connected with each other, that we cannot refuse our assent to parts without discrediting the whole; and since their authenticity is supported by the testimony of so many nations, and such discordant sects; let us firmly believe the truth of this revelation, and return thanks to God, who has not left us to the light of our imperfect reason, but has clearly shewn the way to everlasting life.

THE INSPIRATION OF THE SCRIPTURES.

2 Tim. iii. 16.

All Scripture is given by inspiration of God.

BEFORE we can settle the authority of the Scriptures, it is proper to enquire from whence they are derived; whether from the observation, experience, knowledge, and learning of the writers alone, or from the assistance of some superior being. If they had been composed only by human abilities, the most valuable part of them contained in the New Testament would have been an uncertain and insufficient guide, as the authors were naturally ignorant of many divine truths, full of misapprehensions of the nature of christianity, and must thence have been guilty, without heavenly assistance, of innumerable mistakes. They were indeed

indeed instructed during forty days by our Saviour himself, concerning the meaning of all the facts, of which they had been eye-witnesses, and the application of the ancient prophecies to the events of his life. But so short a time could only qualify them for the office of teachers, when they were supernaturally enabled to recollect all the discourses of our Lord, and could perfectly remember every principal fact of his ministry. By the inspiration then of the Holy Spirit, which was promised by Christ before his ascension, and granted on the day of Pentecost, all their infirmities were supplied, and the weak were enabled to confound the strong. As therefore the authority of the Scriptures depends upon the source, from whence the writers of them drew their information, I shall in my following discourse,

First, shew what increase of wisdom we may suppose the sacred writers to have received from inspiration.

Secondly, defend the history of the Old Testament

Teftament from the charge of fiction or delufion.

Thirdly, anfwer fome objections to the doctrine, that the apoftles were affifted by the fpirit in thofe writings, which were not prophetical.

Firft, I am to fhew what increafe of wifdom we may fuppofe the facred writers to have received from infpiration.

As they were appointed to teach mankind religious truths, and lead them gradually to the knowledge of their Redeemer, the affiftance of Heaven muft be calculated to fupply their own fpiritual ignorance, and make them perfect in all neceffary doctrines. Whatever religious doctrines then we find taught in the Scriptures, we may believe to be true and confiftent with each other; though the types and figures of the law, and even the explanations of the prophets, were far from being equal in clearnefs to the Gofpel. The infpiration of the Old Teftament,
and

and the authenticity of the canon established by Ezra are confirmed by the authority of our Saviour himself; who appeals to the law and the prophets as containing the will of God; and exhorts the Jews to *search the scriptures*, (John v. 39.) that they might discern the justice of his pretensions. Whatever authority then the ancient scriptures had amongst the Jews is confirmed by our Lord. And as they allowed the lowest rank of these to be styled holy, we must conclude, that they were all in general looked upon by the Jews as of heavenly origin. And with respect to the Apostles, as they were the publishers of a better covenant, our Saviour expressly promises them the assistance of the *Spirit*, which should *guide them into all truth.* (John xvi. 13.) Though the Apostles were constant attendants upon our Saviour, during his ministry; though they heard his discourses, and saw his miracles; and though they were instructed by himself, after his resurrection, in the meaning of the ancient prophets; yet they were forbidden to enter upon their office, till they were

farther

farther qualified by Divine inspiration. *Behold,* says he, *I send the promise of my Father upon you: but tarry ye in the city of Jerusalem, until ye be endued with power from on high.* (Luke xxiv. 49.) However low, therefore, we may be inclined to settle the inspiration of the sacred writers, we must suppose them made perfect in the knowledge of such religious truths, as they proposed to teach; or we shall be guilty of gross absurdity in supposing that God neglected to instruct his ministers in the message, which they were sent to deliver. As religion was the business of both the Prophets and the Apostles, they do not seem to have had their faculties enlarged, or their knowledge supernaturally informed in any other matters. But in what was connected with piety or morality, we must either deny all inspiration, or conclude that their doctrines are true, their accounts certain, and their reasoning without mistake. They were not only favoured with heavenly assistance in those truths, which lay beyond the reach of human faculties; but were commanded to rely upon
inspi-

inspiration, where their own abilities might have furnished them with a sufficient, though less perfect defence. *When they bring you unto the synagogues, and unto magistrates, and powers, take ye no thought how or what things ye shall answer, or what ye shall say: for the Holy Ghost shall teach you in the same hour what ye ought to say.* (Luke xii. 11, 12.) But still it does not appear, that this inspiration was ever intended to supersede the use of their reason or senses. It supplied the deficiencies; but left them all the abilities of human nature.

We may therefore safely grant, that the writers of the Old and New Testament were allowed the choice of their own words, provided they expressed the meaning, which was necessary to convey the true doctrines of religion. And we may justly suppose, that where the exercise of reason, or the testimony of the senses were fully sufficient to confirm a doctrine or authenticate a fact, the authority of inspiration might not be superadded. But this is no cause, why we
should

should give up to rash suspicions a great part of the Bible, as false or fabulous, and thence weaken the authority of the rest, with which it is connected. Every part of the scripture does not contain doctrines or facts of equal importance; but we have no sufficient authority for pronouncing any part of it false, or too insignificant for the divine notice. The doctrines of christianity, the predictions of the prophets, and the precepts of the law, which we are informed was *our schoolmaster to bring us unto Christ*, (Gal. iii. 24.) cannot be denied to be of divine original by any, who does not wish to disbelieve all inspiration. And though the historical part of the Old Testament is least connected with religious doctrines, and a narrative of facts, especially delivered by contemporary authors, may deserve full credit without the aid of inspiration; yet let us remember, that the history of Moses is intermixed with the precepts of the law, and that the evangelists relate the discourses of our Saviour, as well as the facts of his life. We cannot perceive in all cases the degree of connection

between

between temporal and spiritual subjects; nor can we decide with accuracy, how far the observation and memory of our Lord's disciples might enable them to give a full account of his actions without divine assistance. But if we believe, that the Scriptures were written to guide us to salvation, and that God always proportions the means to the end; it naturally follows, that the benefit of inspiration was granted to the prophets and apostles in every point, which concerned religion, where their own abilities were insufficient.

With respect to the manner in which the minds of the Prophets and Apostles were affected by Divine inspiration, as we are favoured with nothing similar at this day, we must receive our information entirely from the Scriptures, and can no farther rely upon our own conjectures, than as they are supported by their authority. But by the help of their information we may perceive a remarkable difference between the pretended prophets amongst the Heathen and the servants

vants of the true God, both in the methods, which they made use of to procure the favour of Heaven, and the effects, which inspiration was supposed to have upon their rational faculties. The prophets of Baal *cut themselves with knives and lancers,* (1 Kings xviii. 28.) when they wanted to obtain his assistance; whereas Elijah invoked the aid of the God of Israel in a short, humble, and rational address, adapted to the capacity of all the people. The Heathens pretended to be worked to an enthusiastic fury, when they foretold by inspiration any future event, and that the words, which they uttered, were the immediate dictates of their god, and spoken without their own consent or inclination. But the true prophets and apostles were left in full possession of all their faculties; unless their mind was for a time oppressed by the splendour of a vision, or their heart overcharged with grief at the prospect of future calamities. Equability of temper was indeed so far necessary to receive the influence of the Spirit, that we find Elisha (2 Kings iii. 15.) incapable of its operation, whilst his

his mind was disturbed even by virtuous anger against the king of Israel. The true prophets were commissioned and enabled to declare the will of God; but they were still left at full liberty to obey or resist the motions of the Spirit. Thus we find that Jonah attempted to flee from the presence of the Lord, and did not perform his message to the Ninevites, till he was terrified into repentance, and made sensible of his folly. And St. Paul informs us, that *the spirits of the prophets are subject to the prophets.* (1 Cor. xiv. 32.)

Whether the inspiration of the Apostles was distinguishable by themselves from the operation of their own minds, seems a question of no importance; since they had abundant evidence of supernatural assistance from the improvement of their knowledge. They had hence a clear and consistent view of the whole scheme of man's redemption. They were able to recollect all our Saviour's discourses; many of which were imperfectly understood at the time of their delivery. They overcame their old prejudices. They
coveted

coveted spiritual instead of temporal rewards; preached peace and benevolence, without aiming at conquest; and equally desired the conversion and salvation of Jews and Gentiles. They had besides, at the first descent of the Holy Ghost, an ocular demonstration, that some superior power operated to *give them a mouth and wisdom, which* all their *adversaries* should *not be able to gainsay, nor resist.* (Luke xxi. 15.) I proceed,

Secondly, to defend the history of the Old Testament from the charge of fiction or delusion.

The history of the Old Testament is of all the sacred writings the least intimately connected with the doctrines of Christianity, and may thence be represented as entirely detached. But as it is confessed to be written by Moses and the prophets, as it was preserved by the Jews amongst their holy books, and affords us examples both of faith and practice, it deserves a candid enquiry, what degree of supernatural assistance may be reasonably

sonably supposed to have been granted to the historical writers, and what credit is due to their own integrity and knowledge.

The inspiration and credibility of the history of the Old Testament has been attacked by the adversaries of christianity with ridicule and contempt, in order to invalidate the rest of the Scriptures; and the plain interpretation of it has been given up by some of its defenders, as not tenable in itself, and as if the truth of the history were no ways connected with the doctrines of religion. But though we meet in the Old Testament with many facts, which are only related to prevent a chasm; yet we cannot admit without strong proof, that the holy penmen would be suffered to mix falshood with the truth. The whole Scriptures have been delivered down for centuries as closely connected with each other. We should therefore be very careful not to discredit any part; unless its falshood could be plainly proved, and its author be convicted of credulity or imposture.

The

The Mosaic account of the creation has been objected to by a late royal author[*], as inconsistent with reason. "My reason "tells me," says the king, "that God sees "all things, and that he is every where; "but the Scripture tells me, that God "searched for Adam in Paradise, and called "to him, Adam, where art thou?" If the Scripture in this passage supposed God to be ignorant of the place, where Adam was concealed, it would no less contradict itself than our reason; since the omniscience and omnipresence of God are emphatically declared by the sacred writers. *Thou art about my path, and about my bed, and spiest out all my ways. For lo, there is not a word in my tongue, but thou, O Lord, knowest it altogether. Whither shall I go then from thy spirit: or whither shall I go then from thy presence? If I climb up into heaven, thou art there: if I go down to hell, thou art there also. If I take the wings of the morning, and remain in the uttermost parts of the sea; even there also shall thy hand lead me, and*

[*] King of Prussia.

thy right hand shall hold me. If I say, peradventure the darkness shall cover me: then shall my night be turned to day. Yea, the darkness is no darkness with thee, but the night is as clear as the day: the darkness and light to thee are both alike. (Pf. cxxxix. 2, 3, 6—11.) *Can any hide himself in secret places that I shall not see him? faith the Lord: do not I fill heaven and earth? faith the Lord.* (Jer. xxiii. 24.) Possibly those, who so highly prize their own natural abilities, are indebted to those very Scriptures, which they affect to despise, for the knowledge of such sublime truths. But Moses no where says, that God searched for Adam. When he had transgressed by eating the forbidden fruit, he was summoned before his Maker, obliged to give an account of his guilt, and forced to condemn himself out of his own mouth.

To this and some other objections of equal weight, concerning the creation and the deluge, a defender of the Jewish and Christian religions answers, by supposing
them

them to be * " the ancient popular tradi-
" tions of the Jews, blended with allegorical
" and hieroglyphical imagery, in which it
" is neither very eafy, nor very material
" to diftinguifh what is fabulous from what
" is true;" though he afterwards admits
them to be " originally founded, like moft
" of the mythological fictions of the Greeks,
" upon real and important facts." All this
is eafily afferted, but entirely deftitute of
proof. The Scripture accounts of the creation and the deluge are delivered by Mofes
as a plain narrative of facts, and connected
with a relation of the names and actions
of the antediluvians, which cannot be per-
verted into allegory and hieroglyphic; but
muft either be true, or a collection of miftakes and falfhoods. The Jews, who came
into Egypt with only feventy perfons, had
not time or leifure to form any falfe traditions before Mofes, which might be called
ancient. For the accounts delivered by
Abraham, Ifaac, and Jacob certainly deferve
a more honourable appellation. Mofes alfo

* Effays, vol. ii. p. 197.

appears too wife a man to be impofed upon by fables, and too religious to deceive pofterity by giving them a detail of important events without foundation, or an allegorical collection of unknown facts, which have never been explained. But if we fuppofe it a real hiftory of the creation, deftruction, and renovation of mankind, it is highly credible and confiftent in itfelf, and fupported by authorities not to be denied by any chriftian. The Mofaic account of the creation informs us, that in the beginning God created the heavens and the earth; that in fix days he by his word reduced the earth into order, caufed it to be inhabited by variety of animals, placed man in a ftate of innocence at the head of the vifible world, and put him in poffeffion of happinefs upon the equitable condition of obeying one eafy command; that man, at the inftigation of our great enemy, rebelled againft his benefactor, and was driven out of paradife, expofed to all the evils, which at prefent abound. And what is there in all this inconfiftent with reafon, or the ftate of the world?

world? Or where will the difbelievers of this account furnifh us with a better from the records of antiquity, or the impartial dictates of found judgment? That God created the world needs no proof. That he made man at firft happy and innocent is perfectly confiftent with our notions of his goodnefs. That difobedience is a crime, and that the world abounds with mifery and evil, cannot be denied. And that man fell from his ftate of innocence, and thus forfeited his happinefs, by his own fault, is more probable in itfelf, than any other account we can find of his prefent imperfection.

Many of thefe articles are mentioned again in other parts of Scripture, and thus confirmed by undeniable authority, being adduced as the foundation of moral and religious duties, or to explain the nature and progrefs of fin. The obfervation of the fabbath is declared by the mouth of God himfelf to be founded on the creation of the earth in fix days. (Exod. xx. 11.) St. Paul not

not only mentions the fact, that *the serpent through subtlety beguiled Eve,* (2 Cor. xi. 3.) as an example that christians were in danger of corruption; but assigns it as one reason, why the woman is inferior, and should be obedient to the man. (1 Tim. ii. 14.) The same Apostle likewise contrasts the fall of Adam with the redemption of Christ; *as in Adam all die; even so in Christ shall all be made alive.* (1 Cor. xv. 22.) And our Saviour forbids a man to put away his wife, because in the beginning *God made* one *male,* and one *female.* (Mark x. 6.) The same doctrine St. Paul inculcates to correct the pride of the Athenians, when he tells them, that *God hath made of one blood all nations of men.* (Acts xvii. 26.) St. John also ascribes the murder of Abel by Cain, to his envious spirit and wicked actions. (1 John iii. 12.) It is not therefore of small importance, whether we believe or deny the truth of this history; since it is closely connected with the Jewish and Christian doctrines. And it is most reasonable to determine, that Christ and his Apostles, though they might speak accord-

ing

ing to popular opinion in articles, which they did not profess to teach, fixed the duties of religion upon the rock of knowledge and truth, and not upon the fluctuating sands of mistake and falshood.

And what do the improvements of modern philosophy oppose to all this? A bare supposition, that evil is necessary to produce good. The Scriptures indeed represent temporal evil as sometimes necessary to bring sinners to repentance; and inform us, that final punishment will certainly await incorrigible sinners. But it wants a reasonable proof, instead of an assertion, that misery is the direct cause of happiness to ourselves or others; or that God would not have exempted his obedient servants from every degree of infirmity and pain. If therefore we reject the Scripture account of the creation, we shall be left entirely ignorant, how the world was formed, and puzzled with vain conjectures about the origin of evil.

With respect to the deluge, the authority
of

of Moses is sufficient to give credit to an account consistent in itself, and where the cause assigned is adequate to the effect. That God is able to alter the laws of nature, or to destroy what he has established, no one can deny, who allows his being and attributes. And that universal wickedness was a sufficient provocation for such a signal vengeance is not incredible to any one, who acknowledges, that God makes an eternal distinction between good and evil, and that he always loves the former, and abhors the latter.

If then the deluge was not a real fact, Moses must either have been deceived himself, or have rashly hazarded his reputation for veracity, by giving a circumstantial account of an event, which had no firmer ground than popular opinion. But tradition alone in those early ages would have prevented surmise and fiction from becoming universal in so few generations. Besides it would have ill become the lawgiver, who forbad all slanders and false accusations,

to

to charge the whole world, except one family, with such complete degeneracy, if they had been composed like other generations of a more equal mixture of the righteous and wicked. For though impiety and idolatry have frequently prevailed to a very great extent; yet the world has never since the flood been so totally corrupt. This history also stands uncontradicted by any ancient writer, and is confirmed both by St. Peter, who quotes it as an instance of God's distinguishing justice, (2 Pet. ii. 5.) and by our Lord, who compares the suddenness of his second coming to the careless state of the world in the days of Noe. (Matt. xxiv. 37.) On such an important subject it is to the highest degree improbable, that they should mention a transaction as an example and warning, if it never existed, but owed its belief to popular opinion.

The history of Sampson is also given up as unimportant, and unconnected with the Christian doctrines. But his prodigious strength, when asserted by a credible author, should

should not be denied without positive testimony of its falshood, or some proof of its impossibility. If we are resolved to believe nothing, which is not agreeable to our own experience, our knowledge will be small, and we shall frequently perceive that it has been very defective. From history, therefore, well authenticated, we derive much information, and we believe, doubt, or deny particular facts, as they are related by persons of more or less credit, and appear probable and consistent from the causes and motives, by which they were produced. Unless then we reject the whole history of the Old Testament, we must grant, that God frequently exerted a miraculous power in favour of his chosen people. This makes it perfectly credible, that he might raise up Sampson to be a temporary deliverer, and that a person of such strength and courage might produce a slaughter, which is recorded as marvellous in the sacred Scriptures.

The history of Balaam, though often attempted to be ridiculed, shews an instance

of

of a conduct too common, a person struggling to reconcile the immoderate love of riches with his duty, and to serve at once God and Mammon. The possibility of the miracle cannot be denied. And the propriety of it may be evident, if we attend to the plain circumstances of the story. The prophet, who came to the king of Moab with a full desire to curse the Israelites, was obliged to bless them three times, to foretel their prosperity whilst they continued righteous, and to prevent any other from attempting to imitate his example, by his last solemn words, *Blessed is he that blesseth thee, and cursed is he that curseth thee.* (Numb. xxiv. 9.) Moses could not in this history follow popular tradition, because it happened in his own time. And it is neither consistent with his morality, that he should establish a fact by his testimony, which he did not know to be true; nor with his sense, that he should make himself liable to be convicted of falshood.

If we then impartially examine the history

tory of the Old Teftament, its authority would be much higher, from the credibility of the writers alone, than thefe vague objections feem to allow. The credit of an hiftorian arifes from his judgment, his defire of fpeaking the truth, and his opportunities of difcovering the real ftate and circumftances of the facts, which he relates. Mofes and the prophets in all thefe refpects have greatly the advantage of profane hiftorians. Mofes is the moft ancient of all writers; and even by the help of tradition might be informed with moral certainty of feveral leading facts, and thus guarded againft the delufions of fiction, and the abfurdities of popular opinion. He was inftructed in all the learning of the Egyptians. He was far advanced in life before he was called to an important ftation; and had fpent forty years in the politenefs of a court, and as many in the folitude of a private retirement. But though he had the experience, he was free from the infirmities of age; fince after he had conducted and governed the children of Ifrael forty years more in the wildernefs,

he

he died in the full poffeffion of all his faculties; *his eye was not dim, nor his natural force abated.* (Deut. xxxiv. 7.) And his defire of relating the truth is manifeft from the candour, with which he recounts his own frailties, and the faults and tranfgreffions of God's chofen people. The prophets likewife in general were pious and virtuous, and often eye-witneffes of the facts, which they committed to writing. To this may be added, that the plainnefs, concifenefs, and connection of the ftory contained in the Old Teftament form a ftrong internal evidence in favour of its truth. Whatever regards religion is related at full length; whilft fuch facts, as tended chiefly to gratify human intereft or ambition, are either omitted, or inferted only to connect the reft. We may therefore conclude, that Mofes and the other hiftorians were favoured with the fpirit of wifdom to felect proper facts; and it is not unreafonable to believe, that their knowledge was increafed by direct infpiration, if the ordinary means of information were erroneous or deficient.

The

The connection between Christianity and the historical part of the Old Testament is also confirmed by our Saviour and his Apostles, who frequently enforce the duties of religion from the facts there recorded. In matters only mentioned by way of illustration in proverbs or parables, the sacred writers may use words in the common acceptation, and allude to facts according to the received opinion, without examining whether they be philosophically true, or adding the sanction of their own authority. But in essential doctrines of religion, and truths which are delivered for our instruction, to suppose, that they taught or encouraged us to believe, what they neither knew nor believed themselves, would be to represent our faith erroneous, defective, and inconsistent; and to leave us in such a state of uncertainty, and so much under the influence of our passions and imagination, as seems impossible in a revelation from a gracious God. I proceed,

Thirdly, to answer some objections to the

the doctrine, that the Apostles were assisted by the spirit in those writings, which were not prophetical.

We are told by a modern author, that " the notion is very erroneous, which is " in general maintained by the professors " of Christianity, that the sacred writings " were composed under the immediate in- " fluence of divine inspiration. This no- " tion," says he, " is highly improbable in " itself, plainly contradictory to the general " tenor of scripture, and wholly destitute of " proof, excepting such as may be derived " from a gross perversion of a few detached " passages*." If this author would have us understand by the immediate influence of divine inspiration, that every word was so directed by the Holy Spirit, that the Prophets and Apostles could have expressed the same meaning in no other phrases, he charges the professors of Christianity with an opinion, which few of any knowledge have entertained. If he intends to allow

---

* Essays Hist. and Lit. vol. i. p. 110.

their inspiration, as far as was necessary for the propagation of the sublime truths of religion, the word *immediate* seems likely to mislead the reader, and favour the objections of the infidel. For the effect and authority of every part of the canonical Scripture with regard to us is the same, whether the sacred writers delivered the truth from their own knowledge, or had their deficiencies supplied from the immediate operation of the Holy Spirit; since those parts, where the positive inspiration of the Holy Ghost, not being necessary, was not vouchsafed, were written however under the controul and direction of the same unerring guide. The whole volume therefore carries the seal and stamp of omniscience, as well where the Holy Spirit, ever present to aid those whom he had previously moved to write, secured them from error in relating what they themselves knew, as where they delivered the immediate dictates of Heaven. Let us then examine more particularly how this author supports his assertions. " The Apostles and Evangelists,"

says

says he, "never pretended, like that great impostor Mahomet, that their writings were dictated by the angel Gabriel, or ever urged the perfection of their own compositions, as a decisive proof of the authenticity of the Christian religion." We may grant, that the Apostles did not make use of the pretence of that impostor. They no where boast, like him, of the purity of their style, as surpassing all other writings. But this affords no proof, that they were not inspired. *We speak,* says St. Paul, *the wisdom of God in a mystery. We have received,* says he again in the same chapter, *not the spirit of the world, but the spirit which is of God; that we may know the things that are freely given to us of God. Which things, also we speak, not in the words which man's wisdom teacheth, but which the Holy Ghost teacheth.* (1 Cor. xxvii. 12, 13.) "The testimony they gave to the truth of Christianity was" not therefore, as this author asserts, "to all intents a human testimony;" though we agree with him in his commendation of their fidelity, integrity, and

and opportunity of knowing the truth. The affertion then of St. Paul, that *all Scripture is given by infpiration of God,* (2 Tim. iii. 16.) the teftimony of the fame Apoftle, that he *received not* the knowledge of *the gofpel of man, but by the revelation of Jefus Chrift,* (Gal. i. 12.) the declaration of St. Peter, that *holy men* of old *fpake as they were moved by the Holy Ghoft,* (2 Pet. i. 21.) and the promife of our Saviour, that *the fpirit fhould guide* the Apoftles *into all truth,* (John xvi. 13.) prove without force or perverfion, that the Scriptures are to be obeyed in all precepts, believed in all their doctrines, and relied upon in every point that concerns religion.

Since then we have fuch fatisfactory proofs from the promife of Chrift and the teftimony of the facred writers, that they were affifted by the Holy Spirit; let us draw our knowledge of religion from the Holy Scriptures in preference to the conjectures of fallible men, fupported only by their own natural abilities or the maxims

of

of philosophy. The things of God cannot be learned without the help of the Scriptures; (1 Cor. ii. 24.) and every doctrine contradicted by them is to be rejected. (Gal. i. 8, 9.) But in them we may find a complete treasure of heavenly wisdom, and a full supply for all our infirmities; since they are *profitable for doctrine, for reproof, for correction, for instruction in righteousness, that the man of God may be perfect, throughly furnished unto all good works.* (2 Tim. iii. 16, 17.

THE AUTHORITY OF THE SCRIPTURES.

JOHN xx. 31.

But these are written, that ye might believe that Jesus is the Christ the Son of God, and that believing ye might have life through his name.

IF we consider man as an accountable creature, it is necessary that he should conform himself to some rule of action. And if we view him as a being, who is able by his conduct to increase or diminish his future happiness, it is proper that he should chuse a true and sufficient rule to direct his ways. The only guides, that we can follow, are our own inclinations arising from the impressions of our senses, the dictates of our reason, the information of other men, whom we esteem wiser than ourselves, and
the

the will of God revealed from heaven. The first alone would be uncertain as a rule; since our inclinations may be either innocent or blameable; consistent with our duty, or seeking the gratification of our own appetites, without regard to the interest or happiness of others. Reason indeed, if unprejudiced, can never approve what is vicious or unjust. But it may be defective; unable to discover certain doctrines, or to point out in all cases, how we ought to reconcile our own interest with the good of our neighbour. And if we had no better guide, our unruly passions would predominate by degrees, and obscure the light of our nobler faculties. Much the same may be said of the information of others. As all men are naturally fallible, we might harden ourselves under that pretence against unwelcome truths, and refuse to hear the voice of the charmer, charm he never so wisely. And as we are never quite certain of their integrity; it requires a previous examination of their motives and principles before they can be trusted. And after all we may be deceived

ceived by adopting their mistakes. The only foundation, therefore, upon which we can build securely, is Divine Revelation. This, though communicated through vessels of clay, proceeds from an unerring and benevolent author. And as this revelation is only contained in the Holy Scriptures, I shall in my following discourse,

First, shew that their authority is supreme and decisive in all religious questions. And,

Secondly, that it is uniform in every article necessary to salvation.

First, I am to shew, that the authority of the Scriptures is supreme and decisive in all religious questions.

As our Saviour, by the confession even of those who deny his divinity and atonement, came to teach mankind the will of God; and as he sent his Apostles for the same purpose, and by virtue of the same commission, we can apply to no other with so great a probability of success, if we desire to learn the words of eternal life. If then we grant, that they had heavenly assistance, we must allow the books of Scripture all the authority, which is claimed by their writers; since otherwise we should accuse the Prophets and Apostles of falsely pretending to a divine commission, or suppose them ignorant of the nature and extent of their message, when it is not denied, that they were sent by God.

The authority therefore of the Scriptures is supreme and decisive to command our faith and obedience, as far as they claim the concurrence of God, and are intended to instruct us in the nature and properties of the subject, concerning which they discourse. Their design is to shew us the way to everlasting happiness. Whatever therefore directly and necessarily conduces to that end, we expect to see explained with all the clearness and precision, which are possible in this state of weakness and probation. By the same rule every other subject

ject will be treated with proportionable accuracy, as it is more or less connected with virtue and religion. Thus the different parts of Scripture are in some measure to be interpreted by different rules. Though it would derogate too much from the credit of their writers, and the honour of that Being, whose will they are supposed to declare, to imagine any part of them false or fabulous; the fruits of rash conjecture, or the creature of a fanciful and weak imagination.

But though the Scriptures are intended to shew us the way to everlasting life; yet they are not confined to a mere detail of moral duties. We have in them a valuable, concise, and useful history of the most ancient times, maxims of prudence with respect to our temporal happiness, a chain of prophecies to gain credit to the authors, doctrines of the divine attributes and other spiritual subjects, which could only be known perfectly by a revelation from heaven, and religious precepts of piety and
morality,

morality, which correct our vicious appetites, instruct our weak reason, and are to be obeyed without murmuring or dispute. These articles are not indeed treated so distinctly, that those books, which are chiefly composed of one subject, contain nothing of the other. From hence we may form a probable argument, that being so frequently intermixed, no part is entirely excluded from the divine direction, though some may stand in little need of supernatural assistance. Let us therefore consider separately each part, and see what authority those will allow, who defend Christianity upon a limited plan, and what we may really attribute to it, by the dictates of reason, and the testimony of scripture.

The authority of the historical books must be sufficient to answer the ends, which were intended by God and their respective writers. They were designed in general to set before us the method of his dealing with his chosen servants, the Israelites, who were rewarded or punished, even in this life,

in

in a peculiar manner; to shew how he interfered with the rest of the world upon extraordinary occasions; and to give an impartial account of the principal persons, who as Israelites or ancestors were connected with our Saviour. God has informed us in the law and the gospel, that he loves virtue, and hates vice. And as he chose the seed of Abraham, for his faith and piety, to be his peculiar people; he has shewed us in this world by their prosperity and afflictions, what will be the event of our good or evil conduct. When they trusted on the Lord, and obeyed his laws, they were victorious over all their enemies, *five of them could chase an hundred, and an hundred put ten thousand to flight.* (Lev. xxvi. 8.) When they were tempted to follow the idolatry and corruptions of their neighbours, they were sold into the hand of the heathen, they were conquered by inferior forces, and brought into the lowest state through *oppression, plague, and trouble.* (Pf. cvii. 39.) But even in this situation, when their own arm could be of no service, if they cried unto the Lord, and

and repented of their sins, he raised them up deliverers, and often restored them by a single victory to their former ease and plenty. The destruction of the whole race of sinners by the deluge, the overthrow of Sodom and Gomorrah by fire from heaven, the conquest of wicked kingdoms, and the pardon of the Ninevites, prove the watchful eye and powerful arm of providence; that there is no safety in a course of sin, and that though God is long-suffering, and commonly gives space for repentance and amendment, yet it will not at last be well with the wicked. But perhaps the greatest use of the historical part of the Old Testament is to excite us to emulate the virtues, by which the patriarchs and other saints were eminently distinguished. The faith of Abraham, the patience of Job, the chastity of Joseph, the zeal of David, and all the other instances of virtue recorded in those sacred books, ought to fill us with shame, if, assisted with superior light, we do not strive to merit God's favour by the practice of that abstinence and obedience, which they performed,

formed, who only beheld their reward in types and shadows. But as perfection does not belong to mere man, we must estimate the goodness of their particular actions by their conformity to the written law; and when we read of their faults and miscarriages, should take greater care, lest we also be surprised into sin, which we here see could sometimes prevail over persons of such faith, zeal, and diligence. And if at any time we unhappily imitate their failings, let us also imitate that sincere contrition, of which we have so many proofs in the case of David; and which we may believe was felt by the rest, whenever they were conscious of any offence. But above all others the example of our Saviour in the New Testament most profitably calls for our study and imitation. He alone could challenge his enemies, *Which of you convinceth me of sin?* (John viii. 46.) and all his dispositions were perfectly pure, and constantly devoted to the will of his heavenly Father. It must therefore greatly tend to exalt our virtue, and preserve us from temptations, if we
carefully

carefully obferve, and ftrive to imitate his zeal, meeknefs, patience, and above all his benevolence, which he recommended and enjoined, as the characteriftic mark of his true difciples.

Another part of the Scriptures confifts of prudential maxims, and recommendations of virtue from its good influence upon our temporal happinefs. *Godlinefs*, fays St. Paul, *is profitable unto all things, having promife of the life that now is.* (1 Tim. iv. 8.) But we are not to conclude from the ufe of thefe arguments, that the authors were ignorant of a ftate of future retribution. From the law of Mofes they had the promife of temporal profperity, and from the covenant with Abraham they had the expectation of the Meffiah, who was to reward the patience and faith of the patriarchs, to purify the houfe of Ifrael, and in whom all the families of the earth were to be bleffed. And therefore the Apoftle adds, *of that which is to come.*

Another part of the sacred Scriptures consists of the writings of the prophets, who were sent to foretel future events, to mark the character of the Messiah, that it might not be successfully imitated, or even fully attempted by any impostor, to warn the people to avoid the divine judgments prepared for their sins, and exhort them to repentance, and more strict observance of their duty. We may remark upon these, that the exhortations and directions are of equal importance with the prophecies, and in consequence equally to be ascribed to the superintendance of God, and equally sanctioned by divine authority. For though the prophets were utterly incapable, by reason alone, to foretel what was to come to pass in distant generations, and might explain by their natural abilities the duties of the moral law; yet in cases of almost universal degeneracy, it required supernatural assistance, to point out the most dangerous transgressions, to settle the bounds of their duty, and to avoid being led astray by popular opinions. The office of a prophet with respect

respect to exhortation often requires gifts not necessary to a common teacher; since the latter is guided by a rule, which he acknowledges to be of greater authority than the dictates of his own learning, experience, and wisdom. When God sends a message to mankind, either of information or warning, we must suppose the messenger sufficiently instructed to deliver it without mistakes. And if we grant, that it contains the will of God, it immediately claims our perfect obedience, and the question how much of it absolutely required immediate inspiration, independent of man's natural faculties, becomes vain and useless. Inspiration is intended to render the weak man perfect, the ignorant wise, and to prevent all possibility of error in religious truths. This infallibility in heavenly doctrines is very consistent with natural infirmities in the common affairs of life. But less than this seems incompatible with any notion of divine revelation.

The doctrines and precepts of the Christian

tian religion, with the history of our Saviour's ministry and the first publication of the gospel, are faithfully recorded in the books of the New Testament. In them only can we find an original account of the life and actions, the parables and other discourses of our Saviour, and the doctrines of the apostles delivered in their own words. The authority of these books must depend upon the natural abilities and fidelity of the writers, and the aids to their imperfections, which they received from above. They were eye-witnesses of the facts of our Saviour's life, their dispositions were sincere and devoted to religion, and they had the promise of our Lord, that he would send the spirit to their assistance, *which should guide them into all truth.* (John xvi. 13.) The religion, which our Saviour had proposed to the Jews mostly in parables, they explained in language as clear as the nature of the subject will admit; and thereby proved that their minds were filled with heavenly wisdom. The epistles contain many sublime doctrines, much reasoning upon the attributes and ways of God, numerous precepts to regulate our conduct, and salutary cautions to avoid those errors, which sprang up even in the time of the Apostles, and infested the first ages of the Christian church. These epistles however, though acknowledged by an author of some late Essays * to be of "apostolical autho-" rity, and to breathe a truly christian and "evangelical spirit," are denied by him in general to be binding upon our faith. "Nothing," says he †, "but the prophecies "contained in those writings, together with "a few passages professedly penned from "immediate inspiration, appear to be, strictly "speaking, of divine authority." The obscurity of the words, *strictly speaking*, is here blameable. They seem to grant, that the writings of the Apostles are not to be looked upon as merely human; and yet leave their authority uncertain, to be heightened or lowered, as may best suit the present purpose. The prophecies are allowed to proceed from inspiration, because they were

* Essay 22.   † P. 421, or 2.

impos-

impossible to be conceived by man without divine assistance. Some doctrines likewise contained in the epistles equally exceed the powers of human nature; and must therefore claim the same original, or be looked upon as rash conjectures, or false opinions. But it is farther objected, that all the epistles were of " an occasional nature, written " at different times, to different societies of " christians, upon different emergencies." Many of the precepts are of a general nature, and equally concern all christians. The necessity of charity, as the grand principle of our actions, obliges us as strictly, as it did the Corinthians. And the relative duties ought as much to be practised in these days, as in the time of the Apostles. The faith and duty of all christians are in general the same; though they may be occasionally placed in very different situations, and consequently called upon to exercise different virtues, or undergo different trials. " But," says he further, " the wri- " ters certainly do not arrogate to themselves " that plenary degree of inspiration, they do
" not

"not exact that blind and implicit acqui-
"escence, which is at present generally
"conceived essential." St. Paul asserts, that *all Scripture is given by inspiration of God*, (2 Tim. iii. 16.) which cannot well be understood in a lower degree, than as far as religion is concerned, and as far as our infirmities would lead us into mistakes. And when, in the seventh chapter of his First Epistle to the Corinthians, he distinguishes with so much care between the inspired commands of our Lord, and his own private judgment, which he thought at the same time conformable to the Divine will, (1 Cor. vii. 40.) we have the strongest presumption, that he meant to stamp all the other parts of the epistles, which delivered doctrines or precepts, with divine authority. The apostles never indeed exacted a *blind* acquiescence; nor did they desire an *implicit* confidence without consideration. We are at full liberty to examine with candour the grounds and evidence of christianity; though it is at our own peril, if we suffer our prejudices or evil affections to impose upon our

judg-

judgment, and mislead us to reject religious truth. But St. Paul was so certain of his doctrine, that he pronounced an anathema even against himself or an angel from heaven, which should *preach any other gospel*; (Gal. i. 8.) and he commended the Thessalonians, that *they received the word, which they heard of him, not as the word of men, but (as it is in truth) the word of God.* (1 Thess. ii. 13.) From his character also we may justly conclude, that he endeavoured to write the same doctrines, which he preached. The assistance therefore of the spirit would be equally necessary, when he instructed his converts by letter, as by word. Some part of the epistles may be needless to us, if we be not in danger of the same false doctrines, which were then taught. But as heresies may revive in distant times, if ever we are in the same circumstances, the epistles are as applicable and useful to us, as they were to those churches, to whom they were first addressed. Every part of the Scripture is not necessary in all times, or to all persons. But as we are certain, that its writers were the prophets,

phets, its authority, when applicable, muſt be ſupreme; as we expect no other diſpenſation, it will never be ſuperſeded; and as all truths are conſiſtent, it cannot be contradicted, and conſequently its teſtimony muſt be deciſive. I proceed,

Secondly, to ſhew, that the authority of the Scriptures is uniform in every article neceſſary to ſalvation.

As we are all *called in one hope of our calling,* and have *one Lord, one faith, one baptiſm,* (Eph. iv. 4, 5.) we may reaſonably expect, that all the prophets and apoſtles will direct us the ſame way to everlaſting life. The whole Scriptures concur in one deſign to point out the ſame Saviour. *The law was our ſchoolmaſter to bring us unto Chriſt.* (Gal. iii. 24.) And the Apoſtles *preached not themſelves, but Chriſt Jeſus the Lord.* (2 Cor. iv. 5.) Accordingly the Scriptures give us a conſiſtent account of the nature of God, the diſpenſations of his providence, and our ſeveral duties; though they

they may describe more particularly different attributes under different dispensations. For when God displayed upon mount Sinai the terrors of his vengeance, and the severity of his justice, he proclaimed his abundant mercy, long-suffering, and loving kindness; and when he gave the greatest proof of his love and compassion, by sending his Son into the world to redeem mankind, he appointed the same to be the judge of all, to reward the righteous, and condemn the wicked. The actual exercise of the divine attributes, especially under the law, is sometimes spoken of after the manner of men. Thus when he changes his method of acting, because we have changed ours, he is said to repent; though *with him is no variableness, neither shadow of turning.* (James i. 17.) But if we rightly interpret such passages, as are written in compliance with our infirmities, the Scriptures give us the noblest and completest image of the majesty, wisdom, purity, justice, and mercy of God, that can be conceived in our present state.

In the mediation and redemption of Chrift there is likewife no difagreement amongft the facred writers. For though feveral diftinct acts, which Chrift was to do and fuffer, are foretold in different paffages, and fome in fuch a manner, as to feem fcarce compatible before the event; yet we fee them all fo completely fulfilled in the gofpel, that no contradiction can now be pretended between the feveral accounts of our Lord's office.

The authority of the Scriptures is likewife uniform in exhorting us to repentance of our evil deeds, and the performance of every virtue upon the nobleft and pureft principles. The Ifraelites were commanded in the law to love their neighbours, and affift their enemies. (Lev. xix. 18. Exod. xxiii. 4, 5.) And our Saviour makes love the root of our duty, and extends its branches to every act of ufeful benevolence. There is no good action forbidden or difcouraged by any of his apoftles; nor any evil principle favoured or allowed. St. Paul obferves,

obferves, (Rom. xiii. 10.) that *love is the fulfilling of the law*, because it *worketh no ill to its neighbour*. St. James (ii. 15, 16.) exhorts to charity, and shews how fruitless are the best wishes without suitable deeds. St. Peter commands us (1 Pet. ii. 1.) to lay aside all malice, and guile, and hypocrisy. And St. John, the beloved disciple of our Lord, employs the greatest part of his general epistle in pointing out the benefits we have received from the love of God, and the returns we ought to make to our brethren in imitation of this example.

It may here be observed, that it does not impeach the uniformity of the Scriptures in point of doctrine and authority, that disputes arose very early in the primitive church, that the Apostles sometimes differed in inclination, and that their private conduct might in some few instances deserve rebuke. Heresies began to spring up from men's prejudices in the time of the Apostles. But we are not thence to conclude, without proof, that their writings, properly under-

understood, afforded any real occasion for difference of opinion. As the office of the Apostles still left them men of like passions with us, and the Christian religion was only meant to check or change our dispositions, where they were prone to evil and disobedience, they were liable to variety of inclinations, and might pursue different means to obtain the same end, when the question did not concern the essentials of christianity. And though the Apostles were secure from all danger of mistakes in their doctrine; yet being equally obliged with their hearers to obey the precepts of the gospel, it required care to withstand temptations, and to keep themselves free from the snares of their spiritual enemy. As indeed their knowledge was perfect, and they had weaned themselves from the pleasures, honours, and riches of this world, hoping for their reward in a future life; and as they had the example of our Saviour always before their eyes, and were filled with the most ardent affection for his person, and zeal for his service, we may expect to find them eminent in every virtue.

virtue. But still they were not free from infirmities, and every action of their lives was not to be copied or commended without limitation. When therefore St. Paul reproved St. Peter (Gal. ii. 14.) for seeming afraid of the censure of men, we cannot conclude, that they differed about the nature or extent of our faith, or that St. Peter was not sensible of the liberty of the gospel.

A difference of doctrine has often been alledged between St. Paul, who attributes justification to faith only, and St. James, who insists strongly upon the necessity of good works to complete the same end. St. Paul denies, that our own works alone could render any man acceptable in the sight of God; and produces the instance of Abraham, who *believed God, and it was counted unto him for righteousness*, (Gen. xv. 6.) to prove, that *a man is justified by faith without the deeds of the law.* (Rom. iv. 3. iii. 28.) St. James asserts, (ii. 17.) that *faith is dead being alone*, and that good works are necessary, whenever we have opportunity, to prove

prove that we are guided by a right principle. But these accounts of justification, when duly examined, will be found to contain no contradiction. The two Apostles may be considered as viewing the same subject in a different, though consistent light; and the doctrine of St. James will only prevent men from drawing false conclusions from the words of St. Paul. The latter indeed not only excludes the works of the ceremonial law from having sufficient merit in themselves to procure our pardon and acceptance; but concludes the Gentiles also under sin, who trusted to such righteousness, as could arise from a strict observation of the precepts of morality. (Rom. iii. 9.) But the Apostle observes, that justification in the sight of God cannot proceed from any thing, that can be performed by an imperfect creature. For *not by works of righteousness which we have done, but according to his mercy he saved us.* (Tit. iii. 5.) St. Paul therefore declares, that faith in God's promises, and consequently in Christ, in whom those promises were fulfilled, is the sole

principle

principle of justification. But as good works, being thus denied to be sufficient of themselves to convey real merit, might easily be misrepresented as totally superfluous, St. James insists upon their necessity to perfect our faith, and prove the sincerity of our dispositions. *If a brother or sister be naked, and destitute of daily food; and one of you say unto them, Depart in peace, be you warmed, and filled: notwithstanding ye give them not those things which are needful to the body; what doth it profit?* (James ii. 15, 16.) But St. Paul gives no encouragement to any kind of licentiousness. He exhorts his converts *not to continue in sin, that grace may abound.* (Rom. vi. 1, 2.) *He kept under his body, and brought it into subjection.* (1 Cor. ix. 27.) *He exercised himself to have always a conscience void of offence toward God, and toward men.* (Acts xxiv. 16.) He recommends a perpetual meditation upon *whatsoever things are just, whatsoever things are pure.* (Phil. iv. 8.) He frequently insists upon the relative duties. And in his Epistle to Titus he gives him this

this charge: *These things I will that thou affirm constantly, that they which have believed in God, might be careful to maintain good works.* (Tit. iii. 8.) And St. James is so far from declaring, that works alone will procure us salvation, that he rests the merits of his own good works entirely upon their union with the christian faith; *Shew me thy faith without thy works, and I will shew thee my faith by my works.* (Ja. ii. 18.) Each Apostle therefore agrees, that faith and works are both necessary to constitute a perfect christian, and that we are justified by *faith, which worketh by love.* (Gal. v. 6.)

From this view of the Scripture we may learn, that its design is to make us wise unto everlasting life. We must therefore conclude, that every religious doctrine may be there found with certainty, and that every part is entitled to that credit and authority, which are due to a book published by the prophets of God. And these cannot amount to less than belief of its truth, and obedience to its precepts.

ANSWER TO OBJECTIONS AGAINST CHRIST'S ATONEMENT.

1 JOHN ii. 1, 2.

If any man sin, we have an advocate with the Father, Jesus Christ the righteous: and he is the propitiation for our sins: and not for our sins only, but also for the sins of the whole world.

HAVING in my former discourses considered the truth, inspiration, and authority of the Scriptures, I proceed now to examine the end or design, for which they were written, which is to instruct and guide us in the way to salvation. If we had continued able by our own faculties to perform the will of God, it would have been sufficient to inform us what we had to do, and set before us the motives to the performance. But as we are naturally in a fallen

fallen state, which tends strongly to blind our eyes, and corrupt our hearts; it is necessary, that we should be likewise instructed, where to apply for sufficient assistance; and useful to know, to whom we are indebted for our restoration to the favour of God, even in those particulars, in which our co-operation was unnecessary and impossible. Our love to God ought to be increased, when we learn, that by his mercy we are recalled from death unto life. And we may with more confidence run the race, that is set before us, when we are informed, that our Saviour has discharged that debt, which we were unable to pay, and redeemed us from the slavery of sin, and the power of the grave. Accordingly the Scripture uniformly points out the Messiah, as the object of the promises and types of the law, the person in whose *testimony was the spirit of prophecy*, (Rev. xix. 10.) and the captain of our salvation, by whose stripes we are healed. This faith seems to have been universally received by all, who admitted the fact of our Lord's crucifixion. But this doctrine of our
Saviour's

Saviour's atonement has lately been ranked amongst the early corruptions of christianity. We grant, that many heresies began very early in the church, and that our great enemy not only sowed tares in the time of the Apostles, but often found fit ground to bring them to perfection. But as numbers of christians adhered for many ages to the truth of the gospel; it is not sufficient to assert, that an established doctrine is a corruption, because many persons are of a contrary opinion, unless it can be fairly proved to have no foundation in the Scriptures. Let us not then be induced by the greatest pretensions to superior knowledge, or the utmost confidence of dictatorial language, to mistake innovation for improvement, or to imagine that novelty in itself has any superiority over established belief. I shall therefore in my two following discourses,

First, examine the objections, which have been made to the established belief, that the death of Christ was a proper sacrifice for the sins of mankind.

Secondly,

Secondly, shew how strongly this doctrine is taught in the Holy Scriptures.

Thirdly, point out what use we may make of the knowledge of this truth, to confirm our faith, and improve our practice.

First, I am to examine the objections, which have been made to the established belief, that the death of Christ was a proper sacrifice for the sins of mankind.

Our adversary * objects to the established belief, " that it debases the doctrine of " the natural placability of the divine Be- " ing, and our ideas of the equity of his " government." The placability of the divine Being is sufficiently manifest in the doctrine of atonement, as this mystery was planned by himself, and the sacrifice of our Redeemer proceeded from his bounty. *God*, says St. John, (iii. 16.) *so loved the world, that he gave his only begotten Son.* And if we try the divine pro-

* Dr. Priestley. Corrupt. of Christianity, vol. i. p. 152, &c.

ceedings

ceedings by our ideas of equity, as an adequate rule without respect to his revelation, we shall frequently be in danger of forming erroneous conclusions. *For my thoughts are not your thoughts, neither are your ways my ways, saith the Lord.* (Is. lv. 8.) We must therefore, upon this, and all other religious questions, endeavour to find out the doctrine of Scripture, and submit without dispute to its authority.

It is farther urged against the doctrine of atonement, " that the principle, upon " which it is founded, is not mentioned in " the Scriptures; that it is only deduced " by inference; that the declarations of " God's mercy contain no such limitation; " that it was never noticed by the patri-" archs and prophets; and that the Jews " upon this supposition would have expected " a suffering, and not a triumphant Messiah." In answer to these objections it may be observed, that if the fact be clearly revealed, we are bound to believe it, whether the reason of the dispensation be declared, or not.

not. An inference drawn directly from any clear text is a just foundation for an article of faith. But Christ is also said in express terms to have been the propitiation for our sins, besides many metaphorical expressions of the same import. The patriarchs and prophets might believe in a Redeemer; though they did not mention it on every occasion. We are told, that Abraham rejoiced to see our Saviour's day. And the doctrine of sacrifice for sin was a significant type of *the lamb* of God *slain from the foundation of the world.* (Rev. xiii. 8.) God may be said freely to pardon our iniquities, when he pardons us not for works of righteousness that we have done, but for his own mercy in Jesus Christ. We cannot therefore conclude, that God would pardon sinners upon repentance alone, without the merits and mediation of a Redeemer; nor can we safely rely upon an argument drawn from the opinions of the Jews and Heathens, the former of whom expected a triumphant, and not a suffering Messiah, and the latter rested with confidence upon their own virtue.

tue. That the Jews in the time of our Saviour should entertain wrong notions of the nature of his kingdom, is not wonderful, as their minds were too much attached to worldly pomp and riches, and they expected the blessings of God to be confined to their religion. St. Paul proves, (Rom. iii. 9. Gal. iii. 22.) that both Jews and Gentiles were under sin by the ceremonial and natural law, and could only hope for justification by faith in Christ Jesus. The terms of our salvation were only figured out in the Old Testament under types and shadows. It is therefore an uncertain method of arguing to determine by our own reason the method of God's counsels, and resist the evidence of every text of Scripture, that does not accord with the manner, which we chuse to prescribe. The opinions of the Jews are of little importance. But, since our Saviour's crucifixion, even they have so far opened their eyes to the true meaning of the prophecies, that they have supposed there will be a suffering, as well as a triumphant Messiah; though there never was any reason to imagine, that God would send two Christs; and we are assured, that the same Jesus, who was crucified, and ascended in glory, will so come in like manner, as he was seen to go into heaven. (Acts i. 11.)

The whole force of this objection from the silence of the Scriptures rests upon two assertions[*], that "the sacred writers, though they often speak of the malignant nature of sin, never go a single step farther, and assert, that God cannot pardon it without an adequate satisfaction being made to his justice, and the honour of his laws and government;" and that "the contrary sentiment occurs every where, that repentance and a good life are, *of themselves*, sufficient to recommend us to the divine favour." If a doctrine be taught in Scripture, in plain words, or by direct inference, it does not become false, or unnecessary to be believed, because the principle is not laid down in such words, as are dictated by human understanding. This would plunge us

[*] Page 155, l. 17.

into perpetual doubt. We should be inclined to believe a doctrine, because it seems to be affirmed by some of the sacred writers, and be persuaded to reject the same, because it is not mentioned upon other occasions. The sacred writers do not barely mention the malignant nature of sin; but add likewise the purity of God, and the mission of Jesus Christ. That repentance and a good life are *of themselves* sufficient to procure God's favour, is neither to be found in the Holy Scriptures in express words, nor by direct inference. They are undoubtedly necessary to perfect our holiness. But faith in Christ is shadowed out in the Old Testament, and revealed in the New, as the means of justification. When God calls upon his people to forsake their iniquities and idolatries, *Return unto me, and I will return unto you*; he not only exhorts them to amend their lives, but to return to his protection, to trust in the promises of the covenant made with Abraham, and to obey the law given by Moses. " All the declarations of " divine mercy" cannot justly be said " to
" be

" be made without reserve or limitation to
" the truly penitent, through all the books
" of Scripture, without the most distant hint
" of any regard being had to the sufferings
" or merit of any being whatever;" when
the cross of Christ is so often mentioned in
the New Testament; and we are said to be
washed from our sins in his blood, (Rev. i. 5.)
and saved *by the baptism of repentance.*
(Mark i. 4. Luke iii. 3.) A declaration of
God upon any particular occasion is seldom
so extensive, or contains such a complete
detail of his will, that we may neglect the
rest of the revelation, and disbelieve every
article not expressly mentioned. Wherever
there is a known law or constitution, every
declaration has reference to it; and all its
promises, threatenings, exhortations, and
warnings are to be understood according to
the terms of the covenant, under which men
live. Thus when the Lord passed by before
Moses, and proclaimed his own attributes,
The Lord, the Lord God, merciful, and gracious, long-suffering, and abundant in goodness and truth, keeping mercy for thousands, forgiv-

ing

ing iniquity, and transgression, and sin, and that will by no means clear the guilty, (Exod. xxxiv. 6, 7.) he did not declare in these words, that he would have no respect to the merit and sufferings of his beloved Son, whom he purposed hereafter to send into the world. The conditions of his forgiveness are not here mentioned; the passage being equally silent as to repentance, as it is with respect to faith. It is only said, that God is merciful and gracious, that is, to the obedient; and by no means sparing the guilty, that is, the disobedient. But who are to be accounted objects of mercy or wrath, must depend upon other parts of Scripture, which more fully declare the laws of God and the means of acceptance. It is also urged, that " we certainly could not be " said to be justified *freely*, if the favour " had been procured by the suffering of ano- " ther person." (Rom. iii. 24. Tit. iii. 7.) But as the whole text is, *being justified freely by his grace, through the redemption that is in Christ Jesus*; (Rom. iii. 24.) the act of another person is certainly declared to contribute

bute to our justification, though the grace of God is given *freely* in opposition to our own merits. *After that the kindness and love of God our Saviour toward man appeared, not by works of righteousness which we have done, but according to his mercy he saved us by the washing of regeneration, and renewing of the Holy Ghost; which he shed on us abundantly through Jesus Christ our Saviour; that being justified by his grace we should be made heirs according to the hope of eternal life.* (Tit. iii. 4—7.)

In like manner, when David applies to the mercy of God in the twenty-fifth Psalm, the motives, which should induce God to forgive, are not fully mentioned. If his silence concerning redemption by the death of Christ be urged as a proof of his want of faith, the same argument might be used against the necessity of repentance or amendment. And if David and all the patriarchs knew, and the rest of the Jews might have known, that God had entered into a covenant with Abraham to bless the world by the

the coming of the Messiah, they might trust to the promises of God, and rely upon his mercy according to those promises, though they did not see with the same clearness, that we do, the scheme of God's providence, and the terms of our salvation. The doctrine therefore of the atonement does not make the Old Testament *an unaccountable book*; since the Jews looked forward to the same Messiah, whom we acknowledge to have come at the appointed time. (Acts xxvi. 6, 7.) And whenever Job, Hezekiah, or others, plead their integrity, it may best be understood to mean their sincerity in wishing to fulfil the law of God in obedience to the terms of his covenant. And in this sense a christian may strive after perfection, whilst he relies upon the merits and mediation of Christ to procure his pardon.

That we should forgive others as we hope to be forgiven ourselves, is next brought as an argument against this doctrine. It is certain, that we are bound to forgive our brother, as it is here urged, upon his repentance,

tance, without any atonement. But it by no means follows, though it is called a necessary conclusion, that the Divine Being acts towards us upon the same maxim. The cases are so widely different, that no conclusion can be drawn from the conduct required of man, to determine the method of the Divine mercy, which flows spontaneously from God's benevolence and compassion. The offences of man against man are the offences of one fellow creature, the offspring of the same parents, against another. But our sins against God include the guilt of rebellion against our maker, and ingratitude to our greatest benefactor. We are commanded therefore to forgive, as we hope to be forgiven. But upon what conditions God will forgive us we must learn from his own revelation, and not from any supposed analogy of motives drawn by our own reason in such different cases.

It is asserted*, that " the parables, by
" which our Lord represents the forgiving

---

* Page 159, l. 11.

" mercy

"mercy of God, are the farthest possible from being calculated to give us an idea of his requiring any thing more than merely repentance on the part of the offender." The design of the parable of the prodigal son, and the master who forgave the thousand talents, with others of the same kind, is to shew the infinite mercy of God, the efficacy of repentance, and the necessity of imitating the divine compassion. Nothing more is required of the offender than faith and repentance, because nothing more is in his power. But a parable, which is intended to shew what we are to do to obtain forgiveness, does not deny that something may be done for us by a spotless mediator, which we sinful creatures were unable to perform ourselves. The doctrine therefore of atonement remains to be decided by other texts of scripture. If it be no where declared in words sufficiently plain, it ought not to be believed. But if it be revealed by any inspired writer, it would be wrong to reject it under the pretence, that it is not shadowed out in parables, where it was not the object.

It is true, that our Lord did not tell his Apostles, when they were in sorrow at his approaching death, in those very words, that " he must die in order to procure the " pardon of their sins." But he had informed them the same night, when he instituted the sacrament as a memorial of his death, that *the cup was the new testament in his blood, shed for many for the remission of sins.* (Matt. xxvi. 28.) This seems an expression of the same meaning, and of equal force. And though it be not repeated in his consolatory discourse to his disciples, and intercessory prayer; yet sufficient is said to destroy the opinion, that repentance constitutes the whole of the christian dispensation. He comforts them with the assurance, that his death was necessary for the coming of the Holy Ghost; that he would return in a little while to their great joy; that he went to prepare for them heavenly mansions;

mansions; and that he had gained a victory over the world, by which he would be able to defend them from oppression. Before his crucifixion he did not indeed so fully explain the scheme of our redemption, as after his resurrection. To the Jews he gave convincing proof by his miracles, that he was the Messiah; and prepared their minds by his parables to discern the nature of the kingdom of God. In like manner he qualified his apostles by degrees to teach others those truths, which they naturally were unable to understand. They were filled with false prejudices of the nature of his office and kingdom, which he suffered to continue in part till after his resurrection. *I have yet,* says he, *many things to say unto you; but ye cannot bear them now.* (Jo. xvi. 12) After his resurrection he explained to them in the prophets all things concerning himself. (Lu. xxiv. 27.) And when he was ascended into heaven, he sent the holy Spirit to *guide them into all truth.* (Jo. xvi. 13.) As therefore it was one part of the office of the Messiah to be *bruised for our iniquities;* (Isa. liii. 5.) whenever

whenever our Lord assumes that character, he should be understood as pointing out the end of his sufferings. And though he speaks of the death of his apostles as similar to his own; that does not prove the former to be equally efficacious. We have so short an account of his discourses after his resurrection, that we can conclude nothing from his supposed silence. What he then explained concerning the prophets, we must chiefly learn from the discourses and writings of his apostles, who were commissioned to preach the Gospel, and illuminated from above with all necessary knowledge.

The apostles are said " to have only cal-
" led upon all men every where to repent
" and believe the Gospel for the remission of
" their sins;" and thence it is inferred, that
" we find nothing of this doctrine of atone-
" ment in the book of Acts." But it ought here to be observed, that when the apostles are admitted to have called upon men to believe the Gospel, they must be supposed to mean all the doctrines, which they were
commis-

commissioned to teach. If therefore this doctrine be contained in any part of their writings, it is included in this exhortation, whether it be expressly mentioned, or not, in their introductory discourse. Whoever was called upon to embrace the Gospel, was called upon to acknowledge Jesus as the Messiah, and that necessarily includes every article of doing or suffering, which the Messiah was to perform. The words expiation, satisfaction, and atonement, may be omitted; but in every discourse of the apostles, the doctrine is delivered, that Jesus is the Christ; and from their own explanations we are authorised to believe, that *he died for our sins, and was raised again for our justification.* (Ro. iv. 25.)

St. Peter is said in his two first discourses to the Jews, " to have painted in the black-
" est colours, the sin of the Jews in cruci-
" fying our Lord, and to have exhorted
" them to repent, and to believe that Jesus
" was the Messiah, for the remission of their
" sins; but not to have said one word of sa-
" tisfaction,

"tisfaction, expiation, or atonement, to al-
"lay any apprehension they might have of
"the divine justice." To believe that Jesus was the Messiah was certainly an article distinct from repentance. And if it be proved from the prophets, and the writings of the apostles, that one part of the office of the Messiah was to expiate our sins by his blood, whoever exhorted the Jews to believe in Jesus, exhorted them to embrace our present faith. The great article of religion, which was necessary to be first taught, was, that Jesus was the Messiah so long expected. But what was his office, and what the benefits of his coming, might be explained at first, or deferred to some other time, as best suited the leisure of the apostles, or the circumstances of their hearers. The Christian religion is of too great extent to be fully taught in a single discourse. It is sufficient therefore that the apostles, on any particular occasion, mentioned expresly or virtually the most necessary articles to draw their hearers from their various errors, and lead them to embrace the Gospel of Christ.

From

From hence we may prove, that when St. Stephen alledges to the Jews from the testimony of Moses, and the evidence of his own sight, that Jesus was the prophet who was to come, and that he was exalted to the right hand of God, he declares him the Saviour in whom we are to trust. "But though he makes frequent mention of his death," says this author, "he says not one word of his being a propitiation for sin." If he had said so in express words, we have no reason to think, that this doctrine would have been allowed upon the authority of St. Stephen by any, who reject it, when asserted by St. John.

Philip is also said "to be silent upon this doctrine, though he had so fair an opportunity of introducing it, when he was explaining to the Eunuch the only prophecy in the Old Testament which can be construed to represent it in that light; and yet in the whole story, which is not a very concise one, there is no mention of this doctrine." The whole account of Philip's meeting with the Eunuch and his conversion is extended to fifteen verses. But his answer to the question, Of whom speaketh the prophet this, of himself, or of some other man? is comprised in one, and may therefore be said to be very concise. *Then Philip opened his mouth, and began at the same scripture, and preached unto him Jesus.* (Acts viii. 35.) The passage in Isaiah evidently describes, under a variety of images, a just person, *who suffers for the iniquities of others, and by whose stripes we are healed.* (Isa. liii. 5.) Philip declares this person to be Jesus. Upon which explanation the Eunuch desires to be baptized, and is allowed to be fit to be admitted into the church, upon professing that Jesus Christ is the Son of God. This proves, that Christ was to suffer by his office; and that a conviction, that Jesus is the Messiah and the Son of God, may arise in the mind of a man desirous of learning the truth from a right explanation of this chapter of the prophet. But we may here observe, that it cannot be proved from this passage, that Philip did not mention propitiation

tiation in the same words as St. John. It is concisely said, that he preached Jesus. But we are not told, what arguments, proofs, or illustrations he used; nor how far he shewed the extent of the christian religion. It may also be remarked, that the true question is not, how often this doctrine is mentioned in the prophecies of the Old Testament; but whether our explanation of this passage be just, and confirmed by the declarations and tenor of the Gospel.

It is asserted, that "St. Peter preaching to "Cornelius is still silent about his fundamen- "tal article of the christian faith." The rock upon which our Lord built his church is, that Jesus is the Christ, the Son of God. This virtually contains all the peculiar doctrines of our religion. And when this was once preached and believed, it followed naturally to instruct the converts, what had been done for them, and what was left for themselves to do. It is also asserted, that "what St. Peter here says may, without "any forced construction, be turned against
"this

" this favourite opinion. Of a truth I per-
" ceive that God is no respecter of persons,
" *but* that, in every nation, he that feareth
" him, and worketh righteousness, is ac-
" cepted of him." How this contradicts the doctrine of atonement is not explained. Probably the word *accepted* is by this author taken in such a sense, as to mean, that in every nation he that feareth God, and worketh righteousness, is sure of salvation without any mediator. But if this had been the case, and the Apostle's meaning, there would have been no occasion for Cornelius, who was pious, devout, and charitable, *to send for Peter to tell him words, whereby he and all his house might be saved.* The truth is, he had made a good use of the means, which he had; and was therefore judged worthy of greater light. St. Peter acknowledges, that such in every nation were so far accepted, as to be fit to be admitted into the christian covenant, without being subject to the yoke of the law. But this proves nothing against an atonement. Cornelius was called upon to become a christian. And the christian religion

religion differs from all others, not in requiring repentance for the remission of sin, but in faith in a master, who died on the cross.

St. Paul is also said " to have treated on " many occasions concerning the death of " Christ, but never with any other view, " than as an event foretold by the prophets." St. Paul undoubtedly calls in the evidence of the prophets to convince the Jews, that Jesus was the Messiah, and that his death was part of the office, for which he was sent. But it does not follow, that the prophets foretold the death of Christ merely to shew their skill in futurity; nor is it fact, that St. Paul draws no inference from the crucifixion to prove that he made an atonement by his blood, and that he is become our Redeemer from sin, and a Saviour to lead us to everlasting life. In his discourse to the Jews at Antioch, he calls Jesus *a Saviour, raised unto Israel according to God's promise.* He calls *the gospel the word of salvation.* (Acts xiii. 23, 26.) And after mentioning

tioning the death and refurrection of Chrift, he tells them, that *through this man is preached unto them the forgivenefs of fins.* " He " fhews the Jews," fays this author, " the " aggravation of their fins, and exhorts them " to repentance and to faith in Chrift, and " nothing farther." We defire to go no farther than faith in Chrift, as this includes a belief of his mediation and atonement. This paffage therefore would alone fhew, that fomething more than repentance is neceffary to forgivenefs; fince that was taught by the law and the prophets, and a believer in Chrift *is juftified from all things, from which* the Jews *could not be juftified by the law of Mofes.* (Acts xiii. 39.) The account of St. Paul's preaching to the Heathens at Lyftra is very fhort. He exhorts them *to turn from idolatry to the living God;* (Acts xiv. 15.) but we are not told, in what manner he opened the doctrines of the Gofpel. At Athens likewife he argued againft the worfhip of falfe gods and idolatry, and exhorted to repentance from the confideration of a future judgment, which he proves from

the

the resurrection of Christ. As at the mention of a resurrection his discourse was interrupted, we cannot say with any degree of certainty, that there would not have been "one word of what we believe to be *the true* "scheme of salvation by Jesus Christ," if the apostle had been suffered to make an end. It is not then proved, that "there is nothing "in these discourses evangelical;" nor that "all is legal and carnal;" since they were addressed to heathens, who were not subject to the Jewish law, and it was never mentioned, as having any force or obligation.

Before king Agrippa, St. Paul says, that *he was judged for the hope of the promise made of God unto their fathers.* (Acts xxvi. 6.) And when he gives an account of his faith and preaching, he appeals to Moses and the prophets for the truth of his doctrine, that *Christ should suffer and rise again.* (Acts xxvi. 25, 26.) All this agrees perfectly with the doctrine of atonement. St. Paul does not assert, that repentance alone will procure the remission of sins; but joins the death and

and sufferings of Christ with the light of the Gospel, and the hopes of salvation.

The account of his discourse at Rome is very short, though he spake *from morning till evening.* (Acts xxviii. 23.) We cannot therefore tell, except by conjecture, in what words, or for what particular purpose, *he expounded and testified the kingdom of God, persuading them concerning Jesus, both out of the law of Moses and out of the Prophets.*

All these passages to an impartial and unprejudiced person are very consistent with the doctrine of atonement; as they preach salvation through Jesus Christ. We cannot therefore grant, that * " the Apostles are ab-
" solutely silent concerning this doctrine,"
or that " in their most serious discourses
" they make use of language that really sets
" it aside." And if they " never once di-
" rectly assert," in those very words, " the
" necessity of any satisfaction for sin, or the
" insufficiency of our good works alone to

* Page 165, l. 1.

" entitle

" entitle us to the favour of God and future
" happiness," in the short account which
we have of their discourses in the Acts; yet
if they plainly teach this doctrine in any
part of their writings, it requires our belief,
as being delivered by the messengers of God.

But we are asked, if we are " to build
" so important an article of faith on mere
" *hints* and *inferences* from the writings of
" the Apostles." Hints and inferences are
improperly joined together. Hints are generally supposed so liable to be mistaken, that
an argument drawn from them, cannot
much be relied on, unless it be confirmed
by plainer passages. But inferences are of
greater or less weight according to the connection between the truths that are granted,
and the conclusions which we draw. We
believe this doctrine therefore not from
mere hints, nor even from strong inferences
only; but from a variety of images illustrating this truth, and direct assertions of
inspired writers.

Having

Having asserted, that he has shewn Christ made no atonement, this author proceeds to point out, "from the language of the naked facts, what the end and use of his death really were, namely, to prove the doctrine of a resurrection to immortal life by his own death and resurrection." We grant, that Christ rose again, and that his resurrection was a principal part of his ministry; as it proved the truth of his pretensions, and that he was not forsaken of his heavenly Father. But this neither contradicts the many texts of Scripture, which plainly express or manifestly allude to his mediatorial office; nor does it shew, why he should be put to a cruel and ignominious death, when he might have equally foretold and expressed his assurance of a miraculous resurrection on the third day, if he had died the common death of all men. Neither does this explain, why Christ crucified was to the Jews a stumbling-block. If his resurrection only is to be regarded, that would have been of the same nature, whatever had been his death. But it was a stumbling-block to

their

their faith; becaufe they expected a conquering and triumphant Meffiah, and defpifed a man of forrows and acquainted with grief. The death of Chrift therefore, as well as his refurrection, is one of the leading facts, which are to explain the defign of chriftianity; and this is to be interpreted by the declarations and doctrines of the apoftles, and not our own unfupported imaginations.

Another manner of forming an idea of what is effential to chriftianity is mentioned by this author. He fuppofes a number of chriftians to be caft upon a remote ifland, without any Bible. Thefe he obferves " would firft forget the apoftolical epiftles, " and afterwards the particular difcourfes of " our Lord. But the laft thing," fays he, " they would retain would be the idea of a " man, who had the moft extraordinary " power, fpending his time in performing " beneficent miracles, voluntarily fubmitting " to many inconveniences, and laft of all to " a painful death, in a certain expectation of " being prefently raifed to an immortal life
" and

" and to great happiness, honour, and power,
" after death; and that these his expecta-
" tions were actually fulfilled. They would
" also remember that this person always
" recommended the practice of virtue." It
is certain, that in such a case, good men
would remember a great part of christianity;
that in a few generations their knowledge
would be much diminished; and that the
most abstruse doctrines would be the soonest
corrupted or forgotten. But it is not evident, that they would remember these particulars of our Saviour's life, and forget
that he is our King and Redeemer. Besides,
the extent of our moral duty would soon
become doubtful to christians in such a
situation. And though their faith would be
acceptable, if they practised in sincerity according to their knowledge; yet we cannot
hence determine that no articles are essential
to our religion, the want of which might be
excused in a state of ignorance; or that
christians under such disadvantages ought to
be represented, as fit to form the standard of
our belief.

It

It is brought as an argument against the doctrine of atonement, that "the true and proper design of the gospel, and consequently of the preaching and death of Christ, was to ascertain and exemplify the great doctrines of a resurrection and of a future state." The true and proper design of Christ's coming was undoubtedly to make us heirs of everlasting life. This is by no means inconsistent with the doctrine of atonement through his blood. He shewed us, that notwithstanding our sins it was possible for us *not to come into condemnation, but to pass from death unto life.* (Jo. v. 24.) But whether we are able to procure pardon, and obtain the high prize of our calling by our own efforts, or require a mediator to reconcile us to God, must be decided by the holy scriptures. The very texts, which are cited by this author, contradict the opinion, that we may rely upon our own merits alone. Two of them require faith in Christ; (Jo. vi. 29. xi. 25.) two others assert, that he brought us life, without naming the conditions; (Jo. x. 10. 2 Tim. i. 10.) and the fifth declares,

declares, that the keys of death and the grave are in his power. (Rev. i. 8.) As one condition of our future falvation is holinefs of life, it is no wonder, that it is frequently mentioned with the death of Chrift. And as he was an example of obedience to the will of God, his death was the greateft proof of his refignation. He likewife fulfilled the law and the prophets, by carrying morality to the greateft extent, and both doing and fuffering all that had been foretold concerning the Meffiah. But all this implies no contradiction, why he might not at the fame time fatisfy the divine juftice by his death. And if the latter is afferted in the holy fcriptures, either exprefsly or by direct confequence, fuch reafoning is only an attempt to fet at variance confiftent truths, and to hide from our eyes, that Chrift was the Son of God, and Redeemer of the world; becaufe we acknowledge him the fon of man, the greateft of prophets, and a teacher of righteoufnefs. The whole of his character illuftrates each part; and whatever is plainly taught in the fcripture we are bound to believe, though it may contradict our prejudices, conjectures, and opinions.

The belief of our church is, that sacrifice under the Mosaic law was appointed to atone for sin, and that this had reference to the only true sacrifice, the Lamb of God; as the ceremonies of the law were *a shadow of things to come, but the body is of Christ.* (Col. ii. 17.) This idea is combated by a variety of arguments, in which a figurative expression seems frequently left unexplained, or dismissed as useless, and without any determinate meaning. Christ is acknowledged by this writer to be often called a sacrifice in the Epistle to the Hebrews, and five times in other passages of the New Testament. But the force of these texts, to prove the atonement, is attempted to be evaded by the following methods.

It is objected to the texts from the Epistle to the Hebrews, that it is the epistle of an unknown writer, for " it is not certain, at

" leaſt, that it was written by Paul." It is delivered down to us by the primitive church, as the epiſtle of one of the apoſtles, probably of St. Paul; and before its authority is ſlighted, it ſhould be proved, that we have not ſufficient reaſon to attribute it to ſome inſpired writer. The doctrines contained in it are confirmed by St. Paul, who expreſsly aſſerts, that *the law was our ſchoolmaſter to bring us unto Chriſt.* (Gal. iii. 24.) It is ſaid " to abound with the ſtrongeſt " figures, metaphors, and allegories." But figures, metaphors, and allegories, are not without meaning. And when that meaning is underſtood, they equally require our belief, as the plaineſt paſſages of ſcripture. It is alſo ſaid, that " the reſt of the paſſages " are too few to bear the very great ſtreſs that " is laid upon them; and that this idea is " only introduced indirectly into theſe texts." But it is our duty to endeavour to underſtand the real meaning of the ſcriptures; and not to expect, that every idea ſhould be conveyed in ſuch a manner, as a prejudiced perſon will allow to be direct, or that a truth
ſhould

should be as often repeated, as may seem needful to our weak apprehensions. If Christ were only once styled a sacrifice, it ought to be explained, how he could be a sacrifice without answering the chief end of such an institution; or we should be led to believe, that our sins were forgiven for the sake of his death, and that we were to be saved *through faith in his blood.* (Ro. iii. 25.)

In contradiction to our translation of Isaiah, *when thou shalt make his soul an offering for sin,* (If. liii. 10.) it is asserted*, that "the death of Christ, though frequently "mentioned, or alluded to, by the ancient "prophets, is never spoken of as a sin offering. "The propriety of our translation," it is said, "may be doubted, or, if it be retained, can- "not be proved to exhibit any thing more "than a figurative allusion." If our translation of this passage be faulty, the error ought to be pointed out, and the true meaning restored. For if the vulgar be taught to set

* Page 184, l. 17.

aside

aside the authority of particular texts, merely because the sense is said to be doubtful, the scripture will cease to be their guide in religion, and they will be carried away by every wind of doctrine, by the deceitful craft of those men, who can most easily impose upon their prejudices and passions. And if it be rightly translated, it is not a bare figurative allusion to the Jewish sacrifices, but a direct assertion, that the death of our Saviour answered the same end, for which they were appointed that were offered to expiate the sins of the Israelites. And consequently, as the blood of bulls and of goats cannot wash away sin, that it did in reality, what they represented in a figure, and that it was the substance, and they the shadow.

It is asserted*, that " the Jewish sacrifices " are no where said, in the Old Testament, " to have any reference to another more per- " fect sacrifice, as might have been expected " if they really had any such reference." To this it may be answered, that the scheme

* Page 185, l. 4.

of God's providence and of our redemption was not fully revealed under the law. The whole world was informed in the person of Adam, that *the seed of the woman should bruise the serpent's head*; (Gen. iii. 15.) and from the time of Abraham, in consequence of God's covenant, his descendants had reason to expect, that *in his seed should all the nations of the earth be blessed*. (Gen. xxii. 18.) But the manner of this transaction was not completely unveiled, till Christ himself brought life and immortality to light. We should therefore search impartially, whether this doctrine be taught in the gospel, and not decide, that it has no foundation, because it is not declared in a particular manner in the law and the prophets.

But it is objected*, that " sacrifice is only " opposed to good works or moral virtue, " whenever it is declared insufficient to pro-" cure the favour of God." When sacrifice is declared in the scriptures to be of no value, it is on account of want of sincerity. Sa-

* P. 185, l. 4.

crifice was intended to shew the malignity and deformity of sin, and thence induce men to repentance and amendment. If therefore it is found alone, it is pronounced useless, and even abominable, as leading men to rely upon outward works, without inward purity. It could not in this sense be opposed to the death of Christ; because that is insufficient without the same conditions. Christ came not into the world to excuse the neglect, but to enforce the necessity of virtue. The general strain therefore of the passages quoted above does not appear extraordinary upon the supposition, that the Jewish sacrifices prefigured the death of Christ. And if they did not, this author should declare, what end they were designed to answer; or whether he thinks them useless, though they were appointed by God to expiate sin, as well as to express homage and adoration.

" Many other things," he adds*, " besides
" the death of Christ, are expressly called
" sacrifices by the sacred writers; and chris-

* Page 186, l. 13.

" tians

" tians in general are called priests, as well
" as Christ himself. Why then," it is asked,
" may not the death of Christ be called
" a sacrifice only in a figurative sense?"
The former are evidently figures; but the
same cannot be said of the latter. The
question must therefore be determined by
the general tenor of scripture, and the use
of the Jewish sacrifices upon each supposition.

Many figures are undoubtedly used in the
writings of the Apostles. But whether
Christ, who promoted the reformation of
the world by his doctrines, should only
figuratively be called a sacrifice for the sins
of men by a real death; or whether the word
is to be taken in a literal sense, must depend
upon the nature and circumstances of our
Saviour's death, compared with the doctrines
of scripture. When the literal acceptation
is supported by the same idea being represented under various images of deliverance
from slavery, and restoration to life, by the
means of Christ, and he is expressly called
the

the propitiation for our sins, it seems preferable to any other interpretation, which would imply, that the Apostles by their expressions led us into false opinions, and that they obscurely delivered the principal part of their message. For their frequent reference to the Jewish rites is much better accounted for by admitting a real connection between the ceremonies of the law and the christian doctrines, than by supposing that the Apostles remained under the prejudices of education, after they were enlightened by the gifts of the Holy Ghost; since by these gifts they became *scribes instructed unto the kingdom of heaven*, (Mat. xiii. 52.) who could *bring out of their treasure things new and old*.

The death of Christ is said " to want many " things essential to a proper sacrifice for " sin." One only is named, that " it was " not provided and presented by the sin- " ner." But this circumstance can neither be proved essential by reason, nor is it so declared by revelation.

Sacrifices

Sacrifices under the law are supposed by us to prefigure the death of Christ. This idea is combated by asserting, that they are only " gifts or entertainments." But as it is allowed, that they might be used to deprecate the anger of God, or man, they must perform this service, either by their own value as a gift, by expressing our inward disposition, or by reference to some other object. That they were not regarded on their own account, as a gift, is plain from the book of Psalms, where God says, *all the beasts of the forest are mine: and so are the cattle upon a thousand hills.* (Pf. l. 10.) And though repentance was so necessary to accompany sacrifice, that without sorrow for sin the outward act was of no value; yet there is nothing peculiar in this rite to lead us to suppose, that it was appointed as an emblem, means, or pledge of this disposition. It is most natural therefore to conclude with the author of the Epistle to the Hebrews, that it was a type of the true *Lamb of God, which taketh away the sin of the world.* (Heb. ix. 13, 14. Jo. i. 29.) Whether sacrifices were first commanded by God,

God, or invented by man to express his gratitude and homage, is a question of little importance; since sacrifices for sin were commanded by the law of Moses, and forgiveness promised upon the right performance. And though every such sacrifice was an offering or gift, as well as the vows or free-will offerings; yet it differed from them in this, that it had reference to sin, and was followed by expiation, and therefore became a just type of the death of Christ. The practice of the Philistines and other heathen nations of making atonement by offerings of gold, being not commanded by God, is of no weight to determine the present question. And the ceremonies, which were used in this and other sacrifices, are not of much importance; since it is evident, from the very use of language, that a sacrifice for sin, however it might agree in some points with others, must have reference to transgression and forgiveness.

But it is said, that atonement was made by other methods. Phineas made atonement

ment by slaying the transgressors, Moses by prayer, and Aaron by incense. But this is by no means inconsistent with the notion, that the death of Christ is the only true and proper sacrifice, and that the legal sacrifices, and all other religious rites, owe their efficacy to their reference to Christ's blood, which washes away our guilt, and makes us capable of addressing our heavenly Father.

The resurrection of Christ is mentioned as having the same use with his death. It is therefore concluded, that " the death of " Christ is not a proper sacrifice, and that " the forgiveness of sins does not depend on " it only. *He was raised again for our justi-* " *fication.*" (Ro. iv. 25.) The whole passage is very plain, and confirms the doctrine, which it is brought to confute. *Who was delivered for our offences, and was raised again for our justification.* The death and resurrection of Christ are mentioned as two acts, the one of which was the consequence of the other. The death of Christ was caused by our sins. By his resurrection God declared

his

his acceptance of his death, and that the faithful were henceforth juſtified in his ſight.

" The death of Chriſt is ſaid to be often " denominated in ſcripture in a manner in-" conſiſtent with the notion of a proper ſa-" crifice." As no inſtance is given, it can here only be obſerved, that the idea of a ſacrifice is not inconſiſtent with a ranſom, deliverance by victory, mediation, or interceſſion; and that it perfectly coincides with the notion of atonement and propitiation, which we conceive to belong to the office of our Saviour. Our Lord is often ſpoken of in plain language, and often in that which is figurative. And though it is aſked*, " if " one of the repreſentations be real and the " reſt figurative, how we are to diſtinguiſh " among them, when the writers themſelves " give no intimation of any ſuch difference;" it does not follow, as is here aſſerted, that " this circumſtance alone ſeems to prove that " they made uſe of all theſe repreſentations " in the ſame view, which, therefore, could

* Page 192, l. 15.

" be

"be no other than as comparisons in certain
"respects." It is not difficult for common
sense and reason to distinguish from the subject of the discourse and the context, whether a word is used in a literal or metaphorical sense. We are not therefore reduced to any necessity of understanding every thing literally concerning our Lord, and thus giving way to the doctrine of transubstantiation; or resolving the clearest expressions into obscure figures, and representing the peculiar doctrines of christianity as vague and uncertain. It is very unusual in any author to declare, which words are to be taken in a figurative sense; and yet no one complains of obscurity, where metaphors are used with moderation, or despairs on this account of being able to understand his real meaning. Christ is often called a sacrifice in the New Testament. If he did not really suffer for the sins of men, it should be satisfactorily shewn, in what respects the comparison holds. And if sin offerings under the law had no other reference to forgiveness and transgression than to express that homage and gratitude,

gratitude, which was signified by every other offering that bore a different name, we want a reason, why God appointed a bloody sacrifice, for the reconciliation of sinners. I shall therefore conclude this head and my present discourse with observing, that the scriptures are not silent concerning the atonement of our Saviour; since it was shadowed out by the sacrifices of the law, and the Apostles in all their discourses proclaimed him the Messiah, of whom Isaiah prophesied, that by his stripes we are healed.

THE PROOFS AND USES OF CHRIST'S ATONEMENT.

1 JOHN ii. 1, 2.

If any man sin, we have an advocate with the Father, Jesus Christ the righteous: and he is the propitiation for our sins: and not for our sins only, but also for the sins of the whole world.

HAVING examined, in a former discourse upon these words, the objections, which have been made to the established belief, that the death of Christ was a proper sacrifice for the sins of mankind, I proceed,

Secondly, to shew, how strongly this doctrine is taught in the holy scriptures.

The belief of our church is, that Jesus Christ, the only begotten Son of God, descended from heaven, and was incarnate of the Virgin Mary; that the end of his coming was to appease the wrath of God by his sufferings, to instruct us perfectly in our duty, to procure us grace to walk in the right path, if we be not wanting to ourselves, and to set us an example of patience, humility, benevolence, and all other virtues. Our adversaries grant him to be a true prophet and righteous man; they do not deny the excellence of his precepts, and seem willing to allow him some authority as a lawgiver. But whilst they do not define the extent of his power, nor admit that his commission was to ratify a new covenant, they weaken the strict obligation of his commands, and render his doctrines liable to be slighted. But the denial of his atonement strikes at the very foundation of Christianity, as believed and professed by all other parties. Let us therefore impartially examine, whether the scriptures give us reason to regard Jesus as the Saviour and Redeemer of mankind by the

the offering of his blood, and the sacrifice of himself; or whether he was only a prophet of great power and dignity, and the notion of his atonement introduced into the church after the death of the apostles.

When the angel informed Joseph of the purity of the Virgin Mary, and of her divine conception, he ordered him to call the child that should be born of her by the name of Jesus, because he should save his people from their sins. In like manner St. John saluted him as the Messiah: *Behold the Lamb of God, that taketh away the sin of the world.* (Jo. i. 29.) Isaiah also prophesied, that he should *be wounded for our transgressions, and bruised for our iniquities, that the chastisement of our peace should be upon him, and with his stripes we should be healed.* (If. liii. 5.) Christ himself declares, that *he would give his flesh for the life of the world.* (Jo. vi. 51.) The author of the Epistle to the Hebrews asserts the necessity of a sacrifice for the pardon of sinners, or that *without shedding of blood there is no remission.* (Heb. ix. 22.)

And St. John expressly informs us, that our Lord is *the propitiation for our sins.* (1 Jo. ii. 2.) This doctrine therefore of atonement is revealed in a variety of expressions, and in as direct terms for that purpose as can be conceived. And it is no sufficient objection, that the word, propitiation, occurs only twice; since every doctrine once plainly revealed is to be received with all faith and humility, unless we pretend to be wiser than the prophets inspired by God.

Besides, the whole tenor of the scriptures shews under a variety of images, that man is fallen from the original righteousness in which he was created, that he is admitted again into a state of probation, and restored to favour and acceptance on account of the superlative merits, intercession, and sufferings of one that is pointed out in divers ages to be our Redeemer. Adam was comforted with the promise, that *the seed of the woman should bruise the serpent's head.* (Gen. iii. 15.) And though the Pharisees might have interpreted this prophecy of some triumphant victory,

victory, that should be gained over our great enemy by a display of power and glory; yet the discourses and conduct of our blessed Saviour ought to convince every christian, that he really triumphed over sin and the grave by his death and resurrection.

A plain allusion likewise to the sacrifice of Christ is contained in the command to Abraham to offer up his only son. This is the single circumstance recorded in scripture, to which we can refer the words of our Saviour, when he informed the Jews, that *Abraham rejoiced to see his day.* (Jo. viii. 56.) And because he obeyed the divine word without hesitation, he had the glorious promise, which was fulfilled in Christ, that *in his seed should all the nations of the earth be blessed.* (Gen. xxii. 18.) But though Abraham had many other sons after the flesh; yet in Isaac only, in this sense, was his seed called; as from him proceeded the Messiah, who was to rule over and save all the nations upon earth.

The sacrifices of the law, which were offered as expiations, prove the efficacy of our Saviour's atonement. They were appointed by God himself. In their own nature they were utterly incapable of taking away sin. (Heb. x. 4.) They must therefore bear a relation to some other sacrifice. And they cannot be types of any other thing, than the death of Christ. In this view the burthensome ceremonies of the law were very useful, when they kept in memory the promises of a better covenant. But in any other light we cannot see or learn, why God should appoint such a number of rites, which had neither power to promote morality, expiate offences, nor procure his favour, unless they had reference to some other more perfect and spiritual institution.

Christ is acknowledged to be frequently mentioned, as having *died for us*. This is interpreted of his dying on our account, or for our benefit. For our greatest benefit it undoubtedly was; and we may well take it for what it is plainly described in scripture,

ture, the forgiveneſs of our ſins, and reconciliation with God, upon faith and repentance.

But it is farther ſaid [*], that "if theſe words be rigorouſly interpreted, they will only mean, that Chriſt died for us conſequentially, and by no means properly and directly as a ſubſtitute. For if, in conſequence of Chriſt not having been ſent to inſtruct and reform the world, mankind had continued unreformed, and the neceſſary conſequence of Chriſt's coming was his death, by whatever means, and in whatever manner it was brought about, it is plain that there was, in fact, no other alternative, but his death, or ours." We grant that Chriſt came to inſtruct and reform the world, and to perfect the great diſpenſation of God. We grant likewiſe, that the neceſſary conſequence of Chriſt's coming was his death. But this was not the neceſſary conſequence of his coming to inſtruct, but to redeem mankind. Let this author there-

[*] Page 199.

fore shew, why the death of our Saviour was more necessary upon his supposition, than that of any other prophet; or confess, that the intention of our Lord's coming was something more than instruction or reformation. "Nothing," says he, "but declara-
"tions more definite and express, contained
"at least in some parts of scripture, could
"authorise us to interpret in this manner
"such general expressions as the following."
This observation seems evidently designed to persuade the ignorant, that our Saviour is no where represented in plain texts to have made satisfaction or atonement for the guilt of man. But that Christ is the propitiation for our sins is an express declaration to this purpose by St. John. And the same doctrine is taught by a variety of easy figures in many other places of scripture. We are therefore authorised to interpret general expressions alluding to this subject in a similar sense. Four texts are here quoted as insufficient of themselves to prove this doctrine. *I am the good shepherd: the good shepherd giveth his life for the sheep.* (Jo. x. 11.) Upon this it is

observed,

observed, that "the shepherd does not die for the sheep, in consequence of a compact," and that "it is no proper parallel to the death of Christ on the principle of the doctrine of atonement." No one, I believe, ever said that it was; or understood it as any more than a comparison expressive of our Saviour's zeal and affection for his flock. This is attempted to be explained as contradictory to our notion of atonement. But the other three are left without the least comment; though of a different nature, being plain assertions. *Greater love hath no man than this, that a man lay down his life for his friend.* (Jo. xv. 13.) *Christ hath once suffered for sins, the just for the unjust, that he might bring us to God.* (1 Pet. iii. 18.) This text surely conveys the idea of a pure and perfect Mediator; though it leaves unexplained the terms of the covenant. *It is expedient for us, that one man should die for the people, and that the whole nation perish not.* (Jo. xi. 50.) The high priest himself only meant by these words to advise the death of Christ, as an expedient to preserve the temporal

poral peace and prosperity of the nation. But being by his office, though without his own knowledge, capable of declaring the oracles of God, he prophesies that Jesus should die for the benefit of all mankind. These texts strongly prove, that Christ did something more than preach repentance for the remission of sins, which was done by the Baptist and all the prophets; and that his death more directly contributed to bring life and immortality to light, than theirs, though many of them were martyrs to the cause of truth.

Another idea, by which our redemption is signified, is that of ransom. (Mat. xx. 28. Mar. x. 45. 1 Tim. ii. 8.) This naturally leads us to consider ourselves as in a state of confinement from debt or captivity before the coming of Christ, from which we are delivered by his sufferings and death. It is observed, as before, that " this view occurs " only twice;" though it is confessed that " we meet with similar expressions." It is contended however, that " they must be
" figurative,

"figurative, and signify that he gave his life "a ransom for ours, because nothing but his "mission could have saved the world." That his mission saved us is very true. But this does not prove, any more than the former assertions, that the death of Christ was not literally, properly, and directly the instrument of our redemption. But it is farther observed, that "the price of our redemp- "tion is often said to be given by God; "whereas if we had been doomed to die, "and Christ had interposed and offered his "life to the Father in the place of ours, the "representation might have been expected "to have been uniform." In either case the expressions, though various, may be understood. God *gave* the price of our redemption, because he sent his Son to die for us. Christ *gave* the same price, because he voluntarily submitted to the will of his Father. Both are mentioned to prove the love of God and Christ towards us, and induce us to shew our gratitude by faith and obedience. Whatever representation we may expect, the view, which is offered, seems to prove, that the

death

death of Christ was directly the means of our deliverance from the slavery of sin.

Christ is said *to bear the sins of men.* (Is. liii. 11, 12. 1 Pet. ii. 24. Heb. ix. 28.) This is explained by "taking them away." The word will undoubtedly bear that sense, and in some of the passages that alone. But if we enquire by what means he took away our sins, we shall find it ascribed to his crucifixion. And if we grant, that our sins are taken away, because he died upon the cross; there seems no reason, why we should not acknowledge him as our Redeemer, in the common sense of the word; unless some clear and express declaration could be brought to prove his death necessary upon any other supposition.

We believe Christ to be our Saviour, because we are required to ask in his name. To this it is objected, that " if *all sin* be " forgiven for the sake of Christ only, we " ought at least to have been expresly told " so." And we are expresly told so by St. John

John in the very next verse to that, which is quoted in the page preceding. *If any man sin, we have an advocate with the Father, Jesus Christ the righteous: and he is the propitiation for our sins; and not for our sins only, but also for the whole world.* (1 Jo. ii. 1, 2.) In opposition to the doctrine of the intercession of Christ, it is said, that "the holy Spirit is much more frequently "and properly called our advocate." That both are properly called our advocates we readily believe. But if Christ be not properly our advocate to gain his faithful followers acceptance, it should be shewn, what these texts mean, which certainly ascribe to him some intercession by giving him this title. He confirms and explains this notion, when he assures his disciples, that *whatsoever they should ask in his name,* (Jo. xvi. 23.) they should obtain.

It is observed*, that " our Saviour never
" says that forgiveness of sin was procured
" by him, but he always speaks of the free
" mercy of God in the same manner as the

* Page 205, l. 9.

" prophets,

" prophets, who preceded him; and it is
" particularly remarkable, that in his last
" prayer, which is properly intercessory, we
" find nothing on the subject." Our Saviour
always represents himself as the Messiah;
he proves to the Jews that he had power on
earth to forgive sins, and declares in this very
prayer, *this is life eternal, that they might
know thee the only true God, and Jesus Christ
whom thou hast sent*. (Jo. xvii. 3.) Though
he may not therefore set forth this doctrine
in every place in a particular form, it ought
not to be denied, if it be taught in any
words by him or his apostles. The chief
end of this prayer is to beg prosperity and
protection for his church, whilst on earth.
Christ indeed taught repentance and morality, as preceding prophets had done, though
with more perfection. But he assumed at
the same time much greater dignity; as none
of them called himself the only son of God,
the king of the Jews, or the giver of life
eternal. (Jo. xvii. 2.)

Repentance and remission of sin are said

to be preached *in the name of Christ*, and *through Christ*. From this we may well infer, that he is our Saviour in some peculiar and exalted sense. But this is said to be " easily explained on the idea, that the " preaching of the gospel reforms the world, " and that the remission of sin is consequent " on reformation." All this is positively asserted. But the manner of speaking evidently implies, that remission of sin is owing to Christ in some sense, in which it was never ascribed to any other prophet; since it is preached in his name alone, though they all contributed by their doctrine to reform the world. But it is farther objected, that " had " sin been forgiven in a proper and strict " sense, for the sake of Christ," the word *freely* would hardly have been used. Romans iii. 24. *Being justified freely by his grace.* But the word *freely* means in opposition to our works; and in this very text the redemption of Christ is expresssly mentioned as a cause of forgiveness; *through the redemption that is in Christ Jesus.*

Because

Because "the pardon of sin is represent-ed" in different places, "as dispensed in consideration of the sufferings, merit, life, or obedience of Christ, they are concluded to be partial representations, which at proper distances are allowed to be inconsistent without any charge of impropriety*." This, though darkly expressed, seems designed to take away all meaning from those texts, which ascribe our forgiveness in any respect to Christ. But as the sufferings, merit, resurrection, life, and obedience of our Saviour, all belonged to the same person, and are connected together, we cannot grant any inconsistency in ascribing forgiveness separately to each, as the rest are not thereby meant to be excluded. Christ came down from heaven to save mankind; he preached repentance and obedience, as necessary conditions on our part; and therefore his precepts and example, as well as his death and resurrection, contributed to the reformation and salvation of the world. But it is not "the plain general tenor of scripture," as this author asserts

---

* Page 207.

it to be, "that the pardon of sin is in reality
"always dispensed by the free mercy of God,
"on account of men's personal virtue, a pe-
"nitent upright heart, and a reformed ex-
"emplary life, without regard to the suffer-
"ings or merit of any being whatever*." It
is true, that pardon of sin is always ascribed
in scripture to the free mercy of God; because we can do nothing of ourselves to deserve it. Our personal virtue, though necessary, is no where represented as properly
meritorious. We are exhorted to repentance
and reformation; and, if we obey, and come
to God through Christ, are sure to be accepted. But that God pays no regard to the
sufferings or merit of his Son, is a mere assertion. At his transfiguration the disciples
were commanded to *hear him*, because *he was
the beloved Son* of God. (Mat. xvii. 5.) And
Christ himself says, *therefore doth my Father love me, because I lay down my life, that
I might take it again.* (Jo. x. 17.) The dignity therefore and death of our Saviour are
represented in scripture as essential part of

* Page 207, l. 12.

his mission. These doctrines are indeed frequently delivered in figurative expressions. But the figurative language of scripture as certainly has a meaning as the plainest passages. And till some other meaning be pointed out more consistent, not with men's natural notions of God, which may be defective or erroneous, but with the general tenor of the gospel, we shall believe, that we are *washed from our sins by the blood of Christ*, (Rev. i. 5.) and made joint heirs with him in consideration of his death.

And unless the atonement be the chief article of the christian religion, it does not appear, why St. Paul should *glory in the cross of Christ*. (Gal. vi. 14.) In all things indifferent he made it a rule to comply with the infirmities of men. But though he knew, that this doctrine was *to the Jews a stumblingblock, and to the Greeks foolishness*; (1 Co. i. 23, 24.) yet he esteemed it *the power of God, and the wisdom of God*; and preferred the scheme of God's providence, though slighted by the world, to the boasted wisdom of man's natural abilities. In short, the scripture

ture has a constant eye to this doctrine, and represents the redemption of mankind as the chief end of Christ's sufferings. *Ye were not redeemed with corruptible things, as silver and gold; but with the precious blood of Christ, as of a lamb without blemish and without spot.* (1 Pet. i. 18, 19.) If therefore we disclaim this article, we make a great part of the scriptures unintelligible, and render the reasoning of St. Paul really inconclusive. And if we could persuade the modern infidels to accept such a religion, we should only make them converts to a system of morality, where they would give no credit to its sanctions beyond the dictates of their own reason, prejudices, and passions; and would consequently be involved in all the doubts and uncertainties of the ancient philosophers. Whereas the scriptures were intended to bring life and immortality to light. They shew us a consistent scheme of faith and practice. Their doctrines are capable of being apprehended as to the fact; though the manner of some mysteries may exceed the comprehension of our present faculties. Let us not then prefer darkness to light.

light. But let us rather chuse to be guided by the words of inspired writers, than the most confident assertions of fallible men; and submit our reason to the wisdom of God, rejecting the deceitful systems of human imaginations. I proceed,

Thirdly, to point out, what use we may make of the knowledge of this truth to confirm our faith, and improve our practice.

The attributes of God, as revealed in the scriptures, do not barely increase our knowledge of the nature of the Deity; but rectify and improve those dispositions, which have the greatest influence upon the practice of our duty. Thus the majesty, wisdom, purity, justice and goodness of God, naturally call for our reverence, resignation, virtue, obedience, and gratitude. In the great work of our redemption, what belonged to God alone remains in a great measure a mystery, concerning which *we now see through a glass darkly*; (1 Co. xiii. 12.) and *which things even the angels desire to look into* more perfectly.

fectly. (1 Pet. i. 12.) But what was done upon earth had not only reference to God, as it appeased his wrath, and procured our pardon; but was designed to make us more averse from those sins, which cause our ruin, and to excite us to those virtues, which are necessary to the character of our Lord's disciples.

The crucifixion then of our Saviour proves in the strongest manner the great guilt and danger of sin. The crime indeed of disobeying and offending the infinite majesty of God may be satisfactorily proved by reason alone. And every one is bound to listen to the dictates of his conscience, which, when unbiassed, declares the law of God to be holy, just, and good, and condemns all ungodliness and worldly lusts. But the deductions of reason are sometimes obscure to the ignorant; and often disregarded or forgotten by the negligent, and evaded by the profane. The fact therefore of the atonement, which is recorded in the scripture, sets full before the eyes of the weakest and most thoughtless the greatness of the debt in the value of the ransom; and the ruin, to which we must have been exposed without remedy, if we had not been redeemed by the Son of God. Accordingly St. Paul in his Epistle to the Romans joins those truths together as closely connected. *O wretched man that I am! who shall deliver me from the body of this death? I thank God through Jesus Christ our Lord.* (Ro. vii. 24, 25.)

The crucifixion of Christ, considered as an atonement, proves also the certainty of our pardon. If indeed God had promised by any prophet sufficiently authorized, that he would forgive our offences upon repentance and amendment, we might, without knowing the method of our redemption, have taken it for granted, that he had adopted some means of satisfying his own justice. But though a revelation, accompanied with far less strength and variety of evidence than the gospel, would have demanded our assent; yet, whilst we are in the flesh, it is a gracious condescension in God, that he adapts the

the doctrines of religion to our nature, and not only gives us outward signs of inward grace, but connects the great truths of christianity with historical events, and thus does not confine the knowledge of divine truths to the wise and learned, but makes them plain to the capacity of the weak and ignorant. Thus the crucifixion shews, under a variety of scriptural figures, that our debt is discharged, our ransom paid, and our chains loosed; and the resurrection affords an equal argument, that God has accepted this sacrifice, and enabled the captain of our salvation to triumph over all our spiritual enemies.

The death of Christ, as the cause of our redemption, binds us to the service of our Saviour. *Ye are bought,* says St. Paul, *with a price;* and *being made free from sin, and become servants to God, ye have your fruit unto holiness, and the end everlasting life.* (1 Co. vii. 23.) We should therefore be desirous of learning his will, and obeying his commands, as his service is not only reasonable in itself, but will be attended with the moſt valuable reward. *For the wages of ſin is death: but the gift of God is eternal life through Jeſus Chriſt our Lord.* (Ro. vi. 23.)

Laſtly, our Lord's atonement ſhould ſtir up our gratitude, both to God, who planned and accepted this ranſom for our ſouls, and to our Saviour, who voluntarily for our ſakes drank of this bitter cup. The wiſdom of the ſcheme may ſurpaſs our comprehenſion, and the condeſcenſion of God and Chriſt in vouchſafing to invite the greateſt ſinners to repent and be ſaved, and to pay the ranſom for his murderers and blaſphemers, may appear moſt wonderful, as it is without example. But this is no ground of diſbelief; ſince *God's thoughts are not our thoughts, neither are our ways his ways.* (If. lv. 8.) We ſhould therefore examine the ſcriptures, and readily believe all the doctrines therein contained. And as this is declared and alluded to, through the whole of God's diſpenſations, we ſhould be hence excited to ſhew our gratitude to our Saviour by entertaining

a due

a due sense of his dignity and glory, acknowledging his goodness, and copying his perfect example in such dispositions, as are calculated to bring forth virtuous actions. And if at any time we are called upon to undergo any hardship, or bear any disappointment, for the sake of our duty, let us remember, that he endured the severest afflictions and most painful sufferings for our good, and that we by perseverance are sure to make every temporal evil *work for us* hereafter *a far more exceeding and eternal weight of glory.* (2 Co. iv. 17.)

THE NATURE OF FAITH.

Hebrews xi. 6.

Without faith it is impossible to please him: for he that cometh to God, must believe that he is, and that he is a rewarder of them that diligently seek him.

WHEN we view our own nature, we find ourselves capable of happiness in a greater degree than we ever experience in this vale of sin and misery. Accordingly the scripture informs us, that happiness was the end of our creation, that it was forfeited by man's own fault, and that we are again restored through Christ to a capacity of obtaining the divine favour. But though in
the

the great work of our redemption our Saviour has performed what was not in our power; yet he has not opened to us the prospect of everlasting life without our concurrence. He has shewn us the road to salvation, and promised us sufficient assistance *to run the race that is set before us.* But we must add our own endeavours by the exercise of our reason to discern the truth; and conform our wills to the precepts of our heavenly Father. Full credit should therefore be given to the words of the God of truth, and an entire confidence be placed in his gracious promises. As then faith and obedience are both necessary to form the sincere christian, I shall make them the subject of two separate discourses, and, confining myself at present to the former,

First, enquire what particulars constitute the faith of a christian. And,

Secondly, compare the principal doctrines of the church of England with the tenets of our adversaries, to determine which are most agreeable to the holy scriptures.

First, I am to enquire what particulars constitute the faith of a christian.

The faith of a christian first leads him to acknowledge the truth and authority of the Old and New Testament.

We are not only sensible, that reason alone, besides its weakness, is liable to be misled by our passions and prejudices; but we have positive evidence of various kinds, that God has actually revealed to us his will in the holy scriptures. Whether the whole of the scriptures be the word of an infallible God, and given as a necessary rule in religion to direct our thoughts, words, and actions, or the invention of prudent, though fallible men, is a question of the utmost importance to be rightly decided. If we err by disbelief, we run the risk of disobedience to the will of God. And if we attribute too much authority to the dictates of man,

we

we shall be liable to adopt implicitly his mistakes and impositions. The scriptures are indeed delivered to us by the intervention of men, who were naturally as weak and of like passions with ourselves. But as they certainly received some power from on high, we may reasonably believe, independent of their own testimony, that they were so far strengthened by divine assistance, as to be clear and infallible guides in all things conducive to eternal salvation. For it would be absurd to imagine, that God should in any case propose an end, and leave his instruments unable to produce it. When therefore we find the whole scripture collected by the authority of the Jewish and christian churches, when we find the different parts of the law and the gospel most intimately mixed, and when we find the former as well as the latter confirmed by the authority of our Saviour and his apostles, we must conclude not only that those parts are owing to immediate inspiration, which are expressly declared to be such; but that the general declarations of the divine authority of the scriptures are to be extended

tended to all other passages that regard religion; and consequently that the most positive or specious assertions of human wisdom and learning must be brought to this test, and stand or fall, as they are agreeable or contradictory to the doctrines of revelation.

A firm reliance upon the promises of God, as delivered in the scriptures, is likewise included in the faith of a christian. *He that cometh to God must believe that he is, and that he is a rewarder of them that diligently seek him.* (Heb. xi. 6.) But as we are all sinners, we must listen to the promises of pardon, before we entertain hopes of a reward. *Not by works of righteousness, which we have done, but according to his mercy he saved us.* (Tit. iii. 5.) This pardon is assured to us in Christ Jesus, and we have the farther promise of heavenly assistance to enlighten our minds, overcome our bad dispositions, resist the wiles of our spiritual enemy, and enable us both to will and to do of God's good pleasure. And if we persevere unto the end in a virtuous course, we are certain of being rewarded

warded for ever with glory and happiness far above our present conceptions. *Eye hath not seen, nor ear heard, neither have entered into the heart of man, the things which God hath prepared for them that love him.* (1 Cor. ii. 9.) But when we profess to believe the promises of God, we must believe them in the very sense, in which they are delivered, which is, that we are bound to perform our part by a sincere obedience. We can safely take our notions of the attributes of God only from the scriptures; since if we follow our own imaginations in extending the bounds of his mercy, we may by our ignorance contradict his justice. But if we presume no farther than we are warranted by his own word, we may rely upon his truth and goodness, and our faith will be, in the present life, the substance of things hoped for, the evidence of things not seen.

The last object of our faith is the character of our Lord Jesus Christ, through the various offices, which he sustained upon earth, and the transcendent dignity, to which even his human nature is exalted in heaven. He was a man born of the Virgin Mary. In this respect he endured a life full of hardships and afflictions, and at last, though innocent, was put to a cruel and ignominious death, as a blasphemer against God. He was from the first acknowledged as a prophet and teacher come from God, on account of his miracles. He was likewise that lawgiver promised by Moses to the Israelites to be raised up from among their brethren, (Deut. xviii. 18.) that they might not be terrified by hearing the voice of God, and beholding the majesty of his presence. He was a priest of the order of Melchizedech, that he might offer a more valuable sacrifice than the sons of Aaron, and establish a new covenant upon better promises. He was born king of the Jews to rule in righteousness, and to sit upon the throne of David for ever. But as his kingdom was not of this world, we must farther consider him as our Saviour, who came to redeem us from sin, to reconcile us to our offended Father, and to purify unto himself a peculiar people zealous of good works. And, lastly, he is described in scripture

ture as the only begotten Son of God. All these characters are consistent, and all founded upon plain declarations of holy writ. But it is not to be expected, that they all should be mentioned every time that our Lord is spoken of in any capacity; nor can we justly conclude, that our Saviour's divinity is denied, merely because his human nature is asserted. He is called indeed a man by St. Peter, in his first discourse to the Jews. But he is called *a man approved of God by miracles, and signs, and wonders*; whom *they by wicked hands had crucified and slain.* (Acts ii. 22, 23.) The crime of which he was accused was, that he said he was the Son of God. When St. Peter therefore charges the Jews with wickedness and ignorance, he asserts the divine nature of our Saviour, and calls upon the people to acknowledge him as the Messiah. It is possible to evade the force of many texts, which ascribe to our Saviour the divine attributes, if we obstinately insist, that they are to be understood of him in the lowest sense; because they are sometimes ascribed to others figuratively in similar expressions.

fions. But were it poffible, that each text alone might be underftood in a figurative manner, and a lower fenfe; yet if we have a defire to find the true meaning of the fcriptures, let us ferioufly confider, whether the literal or figurative fenfe be moft proper in thofe paffages, whether they are not applied to our Saviour in far greater number and variety than to any other perfon, and whether our opinion be not confirmed, that he is truly and properly the Son of God, by fome expreffions, which cannot be applied to a mere man without the greateft force.

When we obferve in the Old Teftament, that he is called God in numerous places by the name of Jehovah, and in the New, that the Father is faid to communicate omnipotence to the Son, that he knew what was in man, and that he is called one with the Father on the moft important occafions, and feemingly in the moft intimate fenfe; we ought not to take thefe words in the loweft degree in which they are ever ufed, if we defire, without prejudice, to find the truth;

but

but should rather conclude from such collective evidence, that our Saviour's dignity far exceeded that of all other prophets. And if to these we add, that he is called the only begotten Son of God; that he was conceived miraculously without a human father; that he was not subject to sin, though made like to us in all other things; that he not only existed before his incarnation, but enjoyed with God, before the foundation of the world, the same glory, which he now possesses; that the same Word, which was made flesh, is asserted by St. John to be God; that God by him made the worlds, and has appointed him to be the judge of all mankind; that he is mentioned as an heir by nature, as we, on his account, are by adoption; and that in comparison with him Moses is esteemed only a faithful servant, whilst he is acknowledged as a son in his own house; can we think it probable, that the sacred writers meant to represent him as a mere man? or what stronger expressions could they use, if they intended to make us believe, that he was truly the Son of God in

a sense

a sense superior to all others, and strictly speaking a divine person in unity with the Father? I proceed,

Secondly, to compare the principal doctrines of the Church of England with the tenets of our adversaries, to determine which are most agreeable to the holy scriptures.

The faith of the Church of England in many of the most fundamental articles of religion, is partly or entirely allowed by the church of Rome. They entirely agree with us in the doctrine of the Trinity, and acknowledge the incarnation, atonement, and resurrection of Christ. They do not deny his supremacy over the church, though they suppose him to have delegated such a power to some of his ministers, as gives them a legislative authority of indefinite extent. They grant the scriptures to be the word of God, and allow the necessity both of faith and morality. The sacraments, which we use in obedience to our Saviour, are by them believed to have been instituted by him for the very fame purpose, for which they are applied by the church of England. When therefore we profess so much of what they acknowledge to be the true faith; the articles, in which we differ, ought on their side to be proved necessary and agreeable to the word of God, before they treat us as heretics out of the pale of salvation, and encourage their followers to believe, that our worship is to be avoided equally with death. But the power of the Pope, if they could prove his succession from St. Peter, is not settled consistently by their own writers. His claims have been sometimes contradicted and disallowed by general councils. And a modern champion, after he has justly defined the Pope's real power to be what he had from the beginning, leaves the question still undecided by confessing, that it is impossible clearly to define what acts of his jurisdiction were granted by our Saviour, and what were founded upon human concessions. Transubstantiation also, which formerly was looked upon as the test of their faith, is now explained away into a doctrine, which equal-

ly

ly contradicts the decision of the council of Trent, as it does the opinion of the church of England. And if there should be an invisible change in the sacramental elements, we might reasonably expect to reap the same benefit; as our ministers derive their authority from the apostles, by a succession equally regular, as we consecrate the elements for the same purpose of spiritual sustenance, and fix our faith and hopes upon the same Saviour. Let them therefore shew where we are commanded in the holy scriptures to accept in all ages, and through all changes, the faith of the church of Rome; or prove, that their present belief is conformable to the doctrine delivered by the apostles. The worship of images, the intercession of saints, the use of indulgences, and a few other doctrines, are so far softened and amended in some more enlightened kingdoms, that we might hope for a reformation of their church nearly to the standard of the scriptures, if they would discard their fancied superiority, dismiss their dependence upon what they style a centre of union, and refuse to submit to human authority,

thority, unsupported by divine. But though they now defend these points in such a manner, as to strive to persuade us, that they differ little from our doctrines in this age and nation; yet it is most evident, that their writers formerly recommended superstitious practices to a very great extent; and it is probable, that numbers of their communion remain immersed in bigotry and ignorance; and consequently retain the ancient opinions; whilst they pretend at the same time, that their church is remarkable above others for the unity of its faith.

But some, who approve of the reformation from the errors of popery, think, that the alteration of their doctrines should have proceeded much farther. It is urged, that we are more enlightened in our understandings than our fathers, and that our minds are become free from many of their prejudices. But as they enjoyed the same natural abilities, and professed to be guided by a rational interpretation of the holy scriptures, we should carefully examine, whether any
proposed

proposed change in our faith be agreeable to the word of God, before we proceed to alterations, which may materially affect some essential articles of the christian religion. Freedom from ancient prejudices will not constitute the men of any generation more impartial judges than their forefathers; unless it can be truly asserted, that they have contracted no others equally bad. When we derive our opinions from information, reason, and sense, we may err in either extreme, if we exclude any of these principles from its proper province, or allow it authority beyond its sphere.

With respect to heavenly things, as they are invisible, they cannot be the objects of sense. And reason on that account can only argue by analogy, and draw inferences of their properties from their effects in the creation. The existence, power, and goodness of God are manifest from the things that are seen. But his nature, justice, and mercy must be learned chiefly from what he has communicated of himself by revelation. We

at

at present *see through a glass darkly*, in comparison of that knowledge, when the righteous shall be admitted to the presence of God, and shall *see him as he is*. And if we allow the authority of scripture to be superior to the deductions of reason aided by philosophy, we shall find no sufficient cause to alter the faith of the church of England in essential articles.

The doctrine of our Saviour's divinity has been ranked amongst those corruptions of christianity, which arose from the prejudices of some early converts, who wanted to accommodate the truths of our religion to their former tenets. But St. John, as before observed, who certainly did not borrow his opinions or his language from Plato, says, " the Λόγος was God and was made flesh." Power, majesty, wisdom, and glory are frequently in scripture ascribed to our Saviour in an unlimited manner. For the purpose indeed of our redemption, he put on human nature, in which state he bare our infirmities without our guilt, and was voluntarily

subject

subject to most of the evils and miseries of life, though under the especial care of providence, and promised in all dangers the ministry of angels. But when, besides being called the only begotten Son of God, he is set far above all prophets, by being sent for a much nobler purpose, and made the chief subject of their predictions; and when he is exalted above all principalities, is appointed the final Judge of the whole world, and hath all power committed unto him in heaven and in earth; the language of scripture, concerning his dignity, seems perfectly consistent with his humility and sufferings, on this supposition, and this only, that he united the divine and human nature in one person. The manner and consequences of this union exceed our comprehension. But with our present faculties, *can we by searching find out God? can we find out the Almighty unto perfection?* (Job xi. 7.) For if he was only a mere man, and a mere prophet, commissioned like others to preach morality and repentance, and if he intended to make us rely upon our own merits, and to hope for eternal life as the

proper

proper reward of our obedience; the apostles would seem to have instilled into us very erroneous notions of his nature and dignity. It is incumbent therefore upon our adversaries to explain, how it is consistent with their principles, that such a preference should be given to Christ, as never was attributed to any other mortal; why the most innocent and only perfect man should suffer a painful and ignominious death, if it answered no other purpose than to prove the certainty of a resurrection by his own example; and why we are enjoined faith in him alone, if God had no regard to his sufferings, merits, and mediation. Till these difficulties are satisfactorily removed, we must conclude, that the faith of the church of England upon this article is more agreeable to a plain and rational interpretation of the scriptures; though the doctrines degrading the knowledge, power and authority of Christ, almost to a level with our own, may be more flattering to the pride of philosophy.

How far the doctrines of the scriptures are intended

intended to be represented as uncertain in themselves, or mistaken by our first reformers, cannot yet be determined. But that the opinions received by the church of England concerning the invisible world, and consequently the state of future rewards and punishments, are designed to be weakened, is very evident; since it has lately been asserted*, that " the principle of evil is personi-
" fied, in the book of Job, under the name
" of Satan, agreeably to the oriental mytho-
" logy, in order to obviate the indecorum
" and impiety of ascribing events, apparent-
" ly contrary to the perfection of the divine
" attributes, to the immediate agency of
" God: that the existence of this evil being,
" as a real intelligent agent, is neither an
" article of the Christian nor of the Jewish
" revelation†; and that, however seriously it
" may have been believed by the generality
" both of Jews and Christians, it can claim
" no other credence than is due to an article
" retained from the ancient popular faith,

---

* Essays, Ph. H. and Lit. page 198.

† Page 199.

" originally

" originally founded, doubtless, on the Ma-
" nichæan principles, embraced by the phi-
" losophers of the east."

But if we compare the opinion of the Manichæans with the belief of the Jews and Christians, we shall find, that they differ in important points, and that the latter is well supported by the scripture, and not contradicted by reason. The Manichæans believed, that there were two independent principles, one of which was the cause of all good, and the other of all evil, both natural and moral. But it is false and inconsistent as well with reason as scripture to suppose, that there can be any being independent of God. It is also a mistake to imagine, that any natural evil can be produced without his will and concurrence. *I make peace, says he, and I create evil.* (Is. vii. 14.) *Shall there be evil in a city, and the Lord hath not done it?* (Am. iii. 6.) But the origin of moral evil is best attributed to the perverse abuse of free will; and is uniformly represented in the sacred writings, with respect to man's actions, as
proceed-

proceeding from the suggestions of our spiritual enemy, and the instigation of our own lusts. The personal existence of the Devil is not only probable to those, who allow the possibility of angels, and see the reality of wicked men; but is proved by the testimony of numerous passages of scripture of such various kinds, that they are not all liable to the same evasions. Our Saviour's temptation in the wilderness is expressly recorded. As it was impossible, that he should be internally tempted, who was the only spotless Lamb of God, who did no sin, neither was guile found in his mouth, and whose constant desire in all situations was to fulfil the will of his heavenly Father, we must by all the rules of reason understand the account of the evangelists literally, that he was suffered to be tempted by our spiritual enemy, in order that he might gain a signal victory, and teach us by his own example three important lessons; never to despair of the divine protection, not to expose ourselves to needless dangers upon a false interpretation of God's general promises, and to prefer his service to the acquisition

quisition of all the riches, pleasures, and honours of this world. Our Lord's temptation is compared by this author* "to the "visions of the ancient prophets," and called "a prophetic and divinely instructive "vision imparted to Christ." But such an interpretation should be supported by something stronger than mere assertions. It should be proved, that the expressions ὑπὸ τȣ πνεύματος and εν τῷ πνεύματι convey the same meaning. And it is equally necessary to be pointed out, what instruction Christ would have received from "a scenical representa-" tion of a temptation by an evil spirit," if no such spirit ever existed. The visions of the prophets are related in such a manner, that they can be mistaken for facts only by the vulgar. But the account of our Saviour's temptation is given by the evangelists in such words as naturally convey to all, the idea of a real transaction.

The sacred writers also speak of the Devil as a real person, whom our Saviour came to

* Pages 199, 200.

subdue,

subdue, when they give us an account of our Lord's commission to his apostles. He gave them power to cast out unclean spirits. And when they seemed to rejoice, that the devils, as well as diseases, were obedient to their command, he observes, that he had seen Satan as lightning fall from heaven. Satan cannot by any figure be here put for the principle of evil; since in whatever sense an abstract principle was once in any place, it must remain in the same for ever. But an evil spirit might be created innocent, and admitted to partake of heavenly joys; though it may now be expelled from that seat of bliss for pride, disobedience, or rebellion, and condemned to live in constant terror of the just judgment of the last day. Accordingly St. James represents the evil spirits, as intelligent beings, endued with knowledge, and capable of fear; *the devils also believe and tremble.* (Jam. ii. 19.)

St. Peter also warns us to be *sober and vigilant, because our adversary the Devil, as a roaring lion, walketh about, seeking whom he may*

may devour. (1 Pet. v. 8.) This is evidently not the description of an abstract principle; but of a subtle, malignant, and active enemy, who is perpetually contriving schemes to draw us into error and vice, and thus to reduce us to a level with himself, and accomplish our final destruction.

But the most decisive argument for the personal existence of the Devil may be found in our Saviour's description of the day of judgment. He there informs us, that he will condemn the wicked *to everlasting fire, prepared for the Devil and his angels.* (Mat. xxv. 41.) That the wicked will be punished at the day of judgment no one, that believes the scriptures, can deny. But it is manifest, that the Devil and his angels are here spoken of as equally to be punished with wicked men. These words of our Saviour shew moreover the infinite mercy of God towards mankind, in that he has through Christ offered pardon and salvation to all, and will finally condemn none, but the obstinate and impenitent, who have voluntarily yielded

themselves

themselves servants to sin, and wilfully rejected the means of grace. From all these texts it is evident, that we have a spiritual enemy, who constantly endeavours to draw us from our duty, that christians are concerned to beware of his arts, and that to disbelieve his existence will make us careless in avoiding his dangerous snares, and may have a pernicious influence upon our moral conduct.

Another doctrine retained at the Reformation, which has been lately treated as a corruption of christianity, is the union of the soul with the body, as two distinct principles in the formation of man. It is true, that a resurrection of the body to future happiness might be effected by the power of God, if it were possible, that a thinking animal could be composed of matter alone. And it is likewise true, that we cannot demonstrate how we are made, so as to prove the absolute impossibility of the wildest imaginations, except they contradict the plain meaning of the scriptures. But it is very dangerous,

dangerous, rashly to unsettle men's notions concerning invisible subjects, lest they lose all steadiness arising from first principles. A complete view of the doctrines of the scripture will convince us, that man is there represented as composed of two constituent parts, united in life, and dissolved at death; and therefore that the general opinion of the existence of an immaterial spirit within us is not a corruption of christianity, but a truth consistent with our religion, and probably flowing from the nature of God.

Of all the probabilities, which are the discoveries of reason, or the result of our perception, one of the plainest, firmest, and most universally acknowledged seems to be, that matter is naturally passive, and cannot produce motion, thought, and discourse by any imaginable modification of its parts, without the union or impulse of what we distinguish by the name of spirit. It is to beg the question to suppose matter and spirit to be endued with the same properties, upon the principles of philosophy, unless the fact

were

were supported by the testimony of revelation, or that some particular organization could be clearly pointed out, and proved capable of bestowing the faculty of reason. Men may heap together a number of words, experiments, suppositions, and testimonies, and may affirm or deny at pleasure the properties of matter; but except they can shew the necessity of what they assign as a cause, and its constant connexion with what they assert to be its effect, or rely upon the information, rightly apprehended, of some superior being, whose knowledge is more extensive, their pretended demonstrations will be only conjectures.

But if we will be guided by a fair and reasonable interpretation of scripture, and allow its due authority to the word of God, it is evident, that man is a compound being, consisting of a soul as well as body; superior to mere matter in a principle of self-motion, and distinguished from the brutes in having reason for his guide, and power to pay his Maker a voluntary service. The

very firſt, as well as moſt authentic account, that we have of man, informs us that he was made *in the image of God.* (Gen. i. 27.) This cannot refer to his being formed out of the duſt; ſince God is a ſpirit, and has nothing, which can be imitated by the pureſt matter. The image of God therefore in man appears to be much better explained by the word *ſoul,* as denoting ſomething of a different nature, capable of righteouſneſs and true holineſs, than by any organization of matter. As to the objection, that the ſame word, which is frequently tranſlated ſoul, is ſometimes applied to the dead body, it may be obſerved, that, whilſt we believe man to conſiſt of an union of ſoul and body, we often deſcribe his perſonality by either of them indifferently; and thence it may happen in ſome languages, that the word, which ſignifies the principle of life, may be applied to the perſon of a man, even when dead, provided his perſonality only and diſtinction from others are deſigned to be mentioned, and not an authentic detail given of the whole of his compoſition. Words are
ufed

used both by the vulgar and learned with such latitude, that an argument cannot be properly founded upon the use of a single expression; except where it is placed technically, or with avowed precision. And it is no where declared, that man's being formed of the dust of the earth and becoming a living soul is the whole account of his nature, if we leave out the principal circumstance, mentioned in the former chapter, and explanatory of the rest, that he was created in the image of God. Now that *God is a spirit* (Jo. iv. 24.) we are informed by our Saviour, who thence directs us *to worship him in spirit and in truth*; in opposition to the heathens, who were guilty of offences against morality in honour of their gods, and in distinction from the Jews, who relied upon ceremonies that were only types of inward purity.

And excepting this account of the first formation of man, we have no reason to expect from the scriptures a full revelation of his nature, till the time of the gospel, which

which brought life and immortality to light. Though even under the law Moses cautions the Israelites not to degrade the idea of God by making a material image to be worshipped as a representation of his person or nature; since they saw no similitude, when he descended in glory upon Mount Sinai. But notwithstanding the inferiority of the Jews in religious knowledge, there appear evident traces, that they believed some principle to be in man superior to dust and ashes, and that they expected a more complete discovery of our nature and duty. That death did not destroy the whole man, they must conclude from the appearance of Samuel to Saul, when he foretold his destruction for disobeying the word of the Lord, which could not be known in all its circumstances by any evil spirit. And the very application of Saul to the woman of Endor shewed it to be the general opinion, that something survived the grave. The testimony of Solomon is strong to the same purpose: *Then, says he, shall the dust return to the earth as it was: and the spirit shall return unto God who gave*

gave it. (Eccl. xii. 7.) And it is no contradiction to this, that every imagination of man is sometimes represented as ceasing at death; since an impartial review of those passages would evidently shew, that they mean his worldly schemes and pursuits, or the power of making known the excellence of his Creator amongst mankind.

In the doctrine likewise of our Saviour and his apostles, which contains every article of knowledge that is necessary to salvation, we find two different principles plainly mentioned; one enabling us to receive the knowledge of God, and the other as the chief source of sin and disobedience.

St. Paul makes an evident distinction between the body and spirit in the sixth chapter of his first Epistle to the Corinthians, (v. 20.) where he exhorts his converts *to glorify God in their body, and in their spirit, which are God's.* To assert that our Saviour and his apostles used the word spirit in conformity with popular opinion, though they knew

knew that man had no spirit distinct from the organization of his body, would be to take an unwarrantable liberty with the language of scripture. It is true that the words belonging to other sciences are used by our Lord and the inspired writers in their common acceptation; as the scriptures were neither intended to instruct us in natural philosophy, nor claim any support from its testimony. They are not the wisdom of man; but the power and revelation of God. But in all doctrines, that are necessary to the knowledge of religion, we may depend upon as full an account of every particular, as our nature is capable of receiving at present. When therefore in his Epistle to the Romans (vii. 23.) St. Paul speaks *of a law in our members warring against the law of our mind*, and tells the Galatians, (v. 17.) that *the flesh lusteth against the spirit, and the spirit against the flesh*, and that *these are contrary the one to the other*, he plainly confirms the general opinion of christians, that man is composed of two principles; one of which would acknowledge, that *the law is holy, and the commandment holy,*

holy, just, and good, (Rom. vii. 12.) if the connexion, which it has with the world by its union with the other, did not frequently lead us into temptation.

And that the foul of man is capable of acquiring knowledge by revelation, without the affiftance of the bodily fenfes, is plain from the information of the fame apoftle. *I knew a man,* fays he, *in Chrift, above fourteen years ago, (whether in the body, I cannot tell; or whether out of the body, I cannot tell: God knoweth) fuch an one caught up to the third heaven. And I knew fuch a man, (whether in the body, or out of the body, I cannot tell, God knoweth) how that he was caught up into Paradife, and heard unfpeakable words, which it is not lawful for a man to utter.* (2 Cor. xii. 2, 3, 4.) Had he believed, that a man's body is the whole of his perfon, it appears impoffible that he could have any doubt of the concurrence of his body in this vifion. And if St. Paul had known, that the capacity of thought could arife from the organization of the brain without any other principle, we might

might reasonably expect, that he would not have declared himself a Pharisee, and the son of a Pharisee, without mentioning that they were mistaken in supposing a separate spirit.

The promise likewise of our Saviour to the penitent thief strongly argues the existence of the soul separate from the body. *To-day,* says he, *shalt thou be with me in Paradise.* (Luke xxiii. 43.) This must in our apprehension mean some positive state of bliss; though it may well consist with the full reward of his faith being completed at the general resurrection. To this may be added the difficulty, under which St. Paul declared that he laboured, when *he desired to depart, and to be with Christ, as better* for himself; though *to abide in the flesh was more needful* for his converts. (Phil. i. 23, 24.) If his soul was to rest inactive in the grave, or his power of thinking to be suspended, he might have enjoyed the same reward equally soon, though his life had been prolonged; and we have his own testimony, (Rom. v. 3. 2 Cor. xii. 15.) that he fainted not at tribulation, nor
declined

declined any hardship for the good of the church. Whilst these texts remain, the scriptures cannot be appealed to, as giving no countenance to the doctrine of a spiritual substance united to a material body; since they plainly inform us, that the same man, who was formed of the dust of the ground, was also created in the image of God.

Since then the Church of England acknowledges the scriptures, rationally interpreted, as the sole rule of her faith, and professes to have reformed herself from the errors of the church of Rome by the tenor and authority of the word of God; let us bring all doctrines to this sacred test; and let us neither be charmed with the antiquity of an opinion, if unsupported by the scriptures, nor dazzled with its novelty, if destitute of that foundation. But duly sensible of the weakness of our natural faculties, the obscurity and mysteriousness of the objects of our faith, and the many errors, to which we are liable from our prejudices and passions, let us not be wise in our own conceits, nor lean
too

too much to our own understanding; let us not aim to discover or judge the mysteries of God by the rules of philosophy; and above all let us regulate our hearts and purify our dispositions. If we thus apply ourselves to the study of religion, we may reasonably hope for a blessing upon our endeavours, and an increase of true wisdom; and may in some measure say with holy David, when compared with those, who are careless, or trust too much to their own abilities, *I have more understanding than my teachers: for thy testimonies are my study. I am wiser than the aged: because I keep thy commandments.* (Ps. cxix. 99, 100.)

THE NECESSITY OF OBEDIENCE.

John xiii. 17.

If ye know these things, happy are ye, if ye do them.

THESE words were spoken by our Saviour to his disciples after he had set them an eminent lesson of humility, and exhorted them to follow his example; and they may be equally applied to all his precepts. He came down from heaven to reinstate us in the way of salvation. He procured our pardon upon repentance, instructed us in our duty, and obtained for us the assistance of the holy Spirit. But still he requires our own concurrence, and that our faith and knowledge be perfected by obedience.

ence. I shall therefore in my following discourse,

First, shew what effect the profession of christianity ought to have upon our dispositions.

Secondly, what kind of actions necessarily proceed from a true faith. And,

Thirdly, what care we ought to take to regulate our words.

First, I am to shew, what effect the profession of christianity ought to have upon our dispositions.

As the Gospel discovers the attributes of God in the clearest manner, which we can at present comprehend; the duties arising from our relation to him are equally evident. Reverence naturally arises in our minds upon the consideration of our almighty Creator. And even the wicked have no method of setting themselves free from the awe of the divine

divine presence, except by forgetting the being or true nature of God. In like manner his unexampled goodness displayed in our redemption should dispose our hearts to the most lively sense of gratitude; and both together should beget in us that filial respect, which arises in the breast of a repenting Son pardoned by a most merciful and gracious Father. We should therefore earnestly desire to know his will; study without partiality to understand the true sense of that revelation, which he has compassionately bestowed upon us; habitually prefer our duty to the gratification of our lusts and passions; and admit no comparison between the transitory joys and riches of this world, and our everlasting reward in the next, when they come into competition, and one must be forsaken to obtain the other.

The christian religion contributes likewise to reform our disposition by enjoining a perfect and universal benevolence towards mankind. By sin the soul was made capable of hatred. And all the disturbances that arise in the world proceed at first from our unruly passions. *From whence,* says St. James, (Ja. iv. 1.) *come wars and fightings among you? come they not hence, even of your lusts, that war in your members?* But the fruit of the *Spirit is love, joy, peace,* (Gal. v. 22.) and all the benevolent and amiable qualities. We are not only taught to love men as our brethren, and that God *hath made of one blood all nations, for to dwell on all the face of the earth*; (Acts xvii. 26.) but we are commanded to imitate the divine mercy and goodness; to do good to those, from whom we can hope for no return; and to assist and relieve our bitterest enemies. And that we may never forget our obligation to this duty, we are ordered to offer up our daily petitions for the forgiveness of our own sins upon the express condition, that we forgive others. The rule given by our Saviour for the exercise of our benevolence is both plain and comprehensive. It extends to every thing consistent with justice and our own safety; and applies to our genuine feelings, when divested of partiality. *Whatsoever ye would that*

that men should do to you, do ye even so to them, for this is the law and the prophets. (Mat. vii. 12.) For however covetousness and revenge may harden the heart, when our own interest is concerned; yet compassion and mercy are so natural to the dictates of reason, that no one ever discommended a charitable action, or refused praise to a generous forgiveness of injuries. But though reason approves the exercise of benevolence in all cases; yet our evil passions are so prevalent, that they frequently prompt us to cruelty and revenge. Our Saviour therefore has settled this duty upon the principle of our obedience to God, as well as our relation to mankind; and established it with the strongest sanction; namely, our own hopes of pardon, and future reward. *If ye forgive men their trespasses, your heavenly Father will also forgive you. But if ye forgive not men their trespasses, neither will your Father forgive your trespasses.* (Mat. vi. 14, 15.)

And if we desire to regulate our dispositions, we must make them pure and obedient

ent to the will of God. It is the highest honour to a man to resemble the divine nature. And it is our duty to confine our desires within the limits allowed by our heavenly Father. *Ye shall be holy*, says God to the Jews, *for I the Lord your God am holy.* (Lev. xix. 2.) And our Saviour commands his disciples to be *perfect, even as our Father, which is in heaven, is perfect.* (Mat. v. 48.) For though we cannot attain to the absolute perfection of God; yet we are required, as far as possible, to imitate his purity and goodness. *Know ye not*, says St. Paul (1 Cor. vi. 19.) *that your body is the temple of the Holy Ghost?* Many, who profess our holy religion, seem to form a very wrong standard of christian perfection. If their outward actions appear right in general, or if they are justified by the common maxims of the world, or can be defended by artful palliations, they are satisfied of their own goodness, though they have reason to suspect, that their principles and motives were mixed with evil, and that they would in many cases have been guilty of open acts of wickedness, if leisure, ability,

lity, or opportunity, had not been wanting. Ignorance, indeed and infirmity will be allowed as excuses for numbers of our faults. But these cannot be pleaded, unless we strive to understand our duty, and amend our failings; since we are told by the highest authority, that a settled desire of what is unlawful includes the guilt of a sinful action, and that the precepts, which forbid the greatest degrees of wickedness, forbid all approaches to the same crime. Sincerity then is the test of our goodness. And if we desire to fulfil the will of God, we shall not only lessen the force of temptations, but may by prayer obtain such assistance, as will certainly enable us to go on to perfection. I proceed,

Secondly, to shew what kind of actions necessarily proceed from a true faith.

And, first, we ought to express our piety by the constant worship of God. From him we received our being, with all the blessings of life. To his protection we are indebted in every situation for safety and deliverance. And to his bounty we owe all our hopes of future reward. The evils of this life are inflicted as trials of our faith, or chastisements for our sins, and may all therefore work for our good, if they bring us to due consideration and amendment, by averting our punishment and increasing our reward. If then we consider God as our Creator, Benefactor, King, and Judge, we must pay him our constant tribute of praise and thanksgiving; we must apply to him for help in every distress; and strive earnestly to learn his will, that we may prove our gratitude by a filial obedience. The duty of prayer is so evident, that it cannot be denied, except men avow their disregard of God, and are resolved to follow without controul their wicked imaginations. And if we allow, that men should daily look up to their heavenly Father in their secret addresses, it necessarily follows, that it is both lawful and expedient to do the same in public upon all stated occasions. It is true, that a lifeless attendance upon public worship is of little service, and that hypocrisy in religion

ligion will add to men's condemnation. But real piety is certainly the beſt foundation for perfection in morality, and the neglect of a due obſervation of the Sabbath, is a very great cauſe of that torrent of wickedneſs and diſſenſion, which at preſent prevails in the world. When men neglect their public homage to God, they will by degrees forget their dependence upon him, and diſregard the laws of juſtice and the duties of their ſtation. Their private prayers will ſeldom long continue, when they have caſt off the outward ſhew of religion. And when they have diſmiſſed the principles of piety, they have got free from the checks of conſcience, which threatens divine juſtice for all ſecret crimes, and are left to the uncertain reſtraint of human laws, the natural rectitude of their inclinations, or the capricious dictates of honour. An individual without a due ſenſe of God is dangerous to be truſted. And a nation, which has generally caſt off his fear, ſeems ripe for deſtruction.

Our duty towards mankind is very eaſy

to be practised in all our actions, if our minds be kept free from envy, pride, covetousness, and other selfish affections, and be filled with that benevolence, which becomes a Christian. When we love our neighbour as ourselves, and are willing to treat him, as we desire to be treated in return, there is no danger, that we should wilfully do him any injury or injustice. St. Paul observes, (Ro. xiii. 10.) that *love worketh no ill to his neighbour: therefore love is the fulfilling of the law.* The same principle will impel us to give him all the assistance in our power, when involved in any calamity, or overtaken by distress. A true Christian, like the good Samaritan, wants no inducement to exercise his charity, beyond his gratitude to God, and the calls of humanity. *If he meet his enemy's ox or his ass going astray, he will surely bring it back to him again. If he see the ass of him that hateth him lying under his burthen, he will surely help with him.* (Ex. xxiii. 4, 5.) He will be ashamed to be deficient in those instances of kindness, which were expressly commanded to the Jews by the law of Moses. And he will

will behave himself towards all the world according to the spirit recommended by our Saviour, and not the false glosses invented by the Scribes and Pharisees. Nothing, in short, can excite his opposition but the defence of his own or others rights. And nothing can raise his lasting indignation, but injustice, oppression, or wanton rebellion.

But there are other evil actions, in which men often indulge with less restraint, because they seem chiefly to transgress against themselves. Such are all breaches of chastity and temperance. These vices, though palliated by the guilty, and passed over by the world in general, on account of their frequency, without due censure, tend not only to the ruin of the sinner himself, but to the diminution of the peace, virtue, and happiness of the world. Adultery is confessedly cruel and unjust. And all slighter offences of the same kind are fitly prohibited by the law of God, as they are not only impurities in Christians, who are the temple of the Holy Ghost, and members of Christ, but hindrances of mar-
riage,

riage, which alone can completely secure the happiness of society by taking due care of the preservation and education of infants, and uniting in additional bonds of friendship the different families of mankind. The intemperate man also destroys his health, wastes his time, weakens his reason, and renders himself an useless or prejudicial member of society. And if it be admitted that chastity and temperance are so necessary to the very being of government, that an universal disregard of these virtues would sink the world into a state of anarchy and barbarity, they must be binding in all cases and upon all persons; unless it could be shewn, that some have a peculiar privilege of disobeying the laws of their Maker. God has indeed favoured particular persons by giving them greater riches, wisdom, and authority than others. But as his laws are founded in purity, justice, and truth, he has given no man, however exalted, a licence to sin; but expects, on the contrary, that those, who are most eminent, should shine as lights in the world, and guide the weaker and more igno-

rant

rant by their good example, in the way of truth, virtue, and happiness. I proceed,

Thirdly, to shew what care we ought to take to regulate our words.

For it is not by our actions alone, that we shew our obedience to the will of God; since our words also may greatly contribute to the promotion of virtue or increase of vice. With our tongues we ought to celebrate the praises of God, acknowledge his goodness, and profess his religion. But where men are not impressed with a due fear and reverence of his Majesty, his holy name is blasphemed by oaths and curses. With respect to men likewise, we are capable of contracting much guilt by false, malicious, and injurious speeches. Our words therefore ought to be carefully guarded; since the influence of our example is often more extensive by them than by our actions. We can exhort, persuade, and sometimes convince men to set God constantly before their eyes, *to do all to his glory* (1 Cor. x. 31.) as much as is in their power, *to follow after the things which make for peace, and things wherewith one may edify another.* (Ro. xiv. 19.) Or we may transgress our duty, and disturb the happiness of individuals by unjust calumny, sow the seeds of hatred and division in families or societies by whisperings and falshoods, or stir up sedition, and strive to overturn kingdoms by undermining sound principles, and filling the minds of the ignorant with false, mischievous, and impracticable notions. And in this instance deceivers have a greater power to impose upon weak minds; because men in general are willing to be flattered with an high opinion of their own wisdom, merit, and importance. They can easily be made to believe, that they are able to conduct the business of the world with more prudence than their present rulers; that they deserve a better lot than Providence has thought fit to bestow upon them; and that they are entitled to controul others, and at the same time to follow their own inclinations with the utmost licentiousness. But if we wish not to be deceived, we should never lose sight fight of two plain maxims; that government and subordination are necessary to society, and that lawful rulers can claim an obedience to their just commands by divine as well as human authority. Let us then, when we are enticed to anarchy, sedition, and rebellion, under the specious pretences of civil or religious liberty, remember the admonition of our Saviour, that *every kingdom divided against itself is brought to desolation*, (Mat. 12. 25.) and the caution of the Apostle, (Gal. v. 15.) *If ye bite and devour one another, take heed, that ye be not consumed one of another*. Every state of life in this world, and every government, contains some evils and imperfections, which by wisdom might be alleviated or removed. But we offend as much against prudence as our duty, if on account of moderate inconveniences we plunge into the miseries of war, famine, and pestilence, and leave our real rights at the mercy of the ambitious, or the discretion of the ignorant. And let the secret movers of sedition seriously consider, that they cannot foresee to what crimes and excesses the rage of an ungoverned

governed multitude may proceed, that the event of human affairs, especially in times of confusion, is very uncertain, and that those who trust most to their own abilities, and lay the deepest schemes for unlawful innovations, are still in danger of disappointment, and may perish like Achitophel, in the midst of their own devices. And if they make use of false pretences or wicked arts, let them reflect, that God sees clearly the thoughts of the heart, that he will judge men according to their real goodness, and not their outward appearance, and that the greatest worldly success will neither compensate for the loss of heaven; nor justify an evil action, and secure the sinner from future punishment.

Since then religious knowledge is of such importance to our right conduct in life and hopes of everlasting salvation; since we have a complete and well authenticated system of all necessary truths contained in the holy scriptures; and since we have the promise of heavenly assistance to enable us to fulfil our duty, if we endeavour to deserve it by faith, piety, and diligence; let us study the word of God, with humility and thankfulness; let us believe his promises with full assurance of hope; let us cultivate our reason by all the means in our power, and draw our principles of religion from the proper sources of divine inspiration; let us so regulate our dispositions, thoughts, and actions, as to make them conformable to the will and commands of our heavenly Father; let us prefer the discharge of our duty to all worldly advantages; let us conscientiously practise the minutest virtues, and carefully guard against the sin, which doth most easily beset us; and fulfilling the relative duties of our respective stations, let us impress upon our minds the advice of the apostle, *Honour all men, love the brotherhood, fear God, honour the king.* (1 Pet. ii. 17.)

THE END.

www.ingramcontent.com/pod-product-compliance
Lightning Source LLC
Chambersburg PA
CBHW020802230426
43666CB00007B/809